MADE OF MAGIC

MICHELLE MARIE KING

MADE OF MAGIC

For permission requests, write to the publisher at: www.michelle-marieking.com

ISBN: 979-8-9993489-0-6

Cover Design & Illustrations by January Jones

Edited by Carolyn Jackson

First Edition

Printed in the United States of America

Contents

For the Next Generation.

To the seekers, the feelers, the cycle-breakers, the ones who carry both the ache and the light.

This is for you.

For every moment you've questioned your worth. For every moment you've felt like too much—or not enough. For the silent battles you fight, the dreams you hide, and the magic you're still learning to believe in.

May you never forget:

You are not here to fit in. You are here to *awaken.* To create a world rooted in presence, not perfection. To lead with empathy, love boldly, speak truth, and *shine anyway.*

You are not a problem to fix. You are a possibility unfolding.

This book was written so you would never again have to walk alone in the dark. So that you would know your pain has a purpose, your voice holds power, and your presence is enough.

May these words remind you of who you've always been—And who you are still becoming.

Preface: The Remembering

There's a moment—quiet, unassuming—when something inside you whispers:

"This isn't who I really am."

It doesn't come from shame. It doesn't scream. It simply... aches.

You might hear it in the stillness after the house goes quiet, when you're surrounded by everything you once thought you wanted. Or in the middle of another achievement, when the applause dies down and you're left with the gnawing question, "Why doesn't this feel like enough?"

For me, that moment came after years of building a brand that was changing lives. Of mentoring teens and young adults. Of showing up, day after day, as the role model I once needed.

I had everything I thought I was supposed to want—Success. Impact. A growing business. A beautiful family. And still, I felt like a stranger in my own life.

I was helping others find their voice while quietly losing touch with mine. I was preaching self-love while outsourcing my worth to productivity. I was mothering a daughter—while still trying to mother the younger version of myself I had abandoned long ago.

I didn't need another title. I needed truth. And I was tired of waiting for the breakdown to justify the breakthrough.

So I got still. I listened.

And for the first time in my adult life, I chose to stop performing and start remembering. Not just who I was before the titles and accomplishments. But who I had been underneath it all along.

That remembering became my rebellion. And, without realizing it...

it also became my magic.

Where the Spark Began

This book was born out of that choice—to come home to myself. Not after everything was fixed or figured out. But right in the middle of the mess. Right when it would've been easier to go numb. Right when I needed something real to hold onto.

That something was my Lifespark—a word I'll come back to again and again in these pages.

It's not a goal. It's not a job title. It's the flicker inside you that refuses to burn out. The pulse of purpose that keeps beating—even when your heart feels broken.

And if you're here, reading these words, maybe you're standing on the edge of that same remembering. Maybe you're exhausted from holding it all together. From being strong, capable, and "fine" while quietly unraveling. Maybe you're successful by every external metric, but still feel like something essential is missing.

Or maybe, like me, you're finally ready to stop shrinking to fit your life—and start expanding into the one that's been waiting for you all along.

If so—this book is for you

The Truth Beneath the Titles

I'm Michelle Marie King - Founder of Positive Presence Global, the largest life coaching company for the next generation. I've mentored thousands of teens and young adults across the globe.

I'm a former international runway model & pageant title-holder, and a nationally renowned motivational public speaker, social entrepreneur, and positivity activist. My favorite titles are mother and wife.

But beneath all of that, I'm just a girl who spent too many years trying to earn her worth. And then one day, I decided to rewrite the story.

This book is part memoir, part mirror. Inside these pages, I'm telling the truth—my truth—so you can begin to tell yours.

You'll read about the collapse of a business and the resurrection of a calling. About trauma that shaped me, relationships that nearly broke me, and the grace that kept whispering, "Not yet. There's more."

You'll meet the woman I've become—yes. But more importantly, you'll meet the girl I returned to. The one who never needed fixing—just witnessing.

This is not a how-to guide. It's a how-it-feels guide. It's about what it looks like to live with your heart open, your truth exposed, and a steady purpose even when your hands are shaking.

And yes—it's about magic. Not the glittery, curated, once-a-year kind. But the everyday, deep soul-defining kind.

The kind you create when you show up fully. The kind that happens when you tell your truth. The kind you remember when you finally stop running from yourself and sit still long enough to feel the authenticity of your life.

That magic started to surface for me as I helped the next generation find theirs. But what I realized very quickly is that they're drowning. Not in apathy—but like all of us—in pressure, shame, perfectionism, and fear.

They don't need saving. They need self-love. An awakening to their uniqueness and inner spark. But how could I teach them how to love themselves... if I didn't yet love who I was?

So I did the work. I got curious. I got quiet.

And then—I let my life teach me what no textbook ever could. This book is what came out of that classroom.

This is Your Moment

If you've ever felt like you had to earn rest, prove love, or perform for peace—This is your invitation to stop.

To return to your story. To honor your sensitivity as strength. To reclaim your voice. To remember your magic.

Because your magic isn't something you lost. It's something you forgot how to believe in. Let this book be your reminder.

You don't need a five-year plan or a perfect morning routine. You need a moment. One breath. One truth. One quiet choice to come back to yourself.

This isn't a manual. It's a mirror. Not here to fix you—But to walk with you.

So come as you are. Messy. Tender. Brave. There's nothing to prove here. Only something to remember.

Welcome home. Let's begin!

1

Finding My Magic

We are all wearing hats. Roles. Labels. Expectations. Whatever you call it, they exist outside of us.

Some were placed on us before we could walk—sister, crybaby, the quiet one. Others we picked up along the way, thinking they'd help us fit in, belong, and feel worthy.

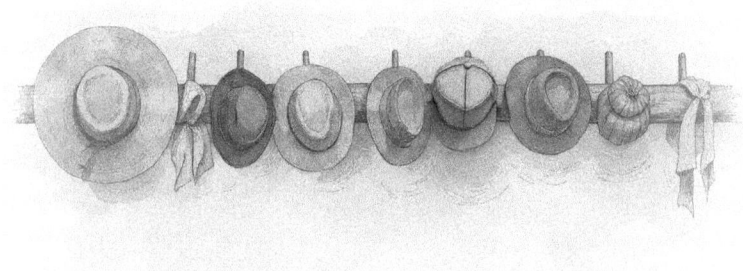

Many were cast upon us as judgment from others: Immature teenager. Dumb blonde. Lazy college student. Superficial model. Inexperienced entrepreneur. Incapable mother.

And those are just the ones I've worn.

We all carry an inner identity—a true self—that often gets refracted, even distorted, through the lens of social conditioning. Over time, we start to mistake one of the hats we wear for the whole of who we are.

We forget we're more than just a single role, label, or expectation. But if we're lucky, something inside us stirs. A quiet rebellion begins—a powerful, gentle uprising of your true self.

This chapter is about that rebellion. About rediscovering that your greatest gift—your magic—isn't something you *find out there*. It's something you *remember in here*.

And for me, that remembering began with a spark.

Finding My Spark

I was fifteen the first time I felt the pulse of something I now recognize as magic.

It was Club Day at my high school—tables lining the cafeteria, students grabbing fliers with half-interest.

I didn't expect anything to jump out at me.

I was short, curvy, with brown, puffy hair and a loud laugh I hadn't yet learned to love.

But then, at one quiet table, I spotted a flier for a youth program called ARCh—the Association for the Rights of Citizens with handicaps.

Me Freshman Year of High School

They performed skits to teach kids about disabilities and differences—about empathy, inclusion, and acceptance.

Something in my chest caught fire. I didn't think, I just walked over and signed up. My feet moved before my fear could catch up.

Looking back, that was the first time I tasted purpose.

For the next three years, I traveled with ARCh all over Wisconsin—performing in elementary, middle schools, and high schools—holding space for connection and kindness. I wasn't the best actor. I wasn't the loudest voice.

But I was alive.

On stage, something clicked. I felt seen, not for how I looked, but for what I carried inside. For the first time, I let my light shine without apology.

My junior year, we were invited to perform at the Inaugural Shaken Baby Syndrome Conference on the steps of the Capitol in Washington, DC, in front of hundreds of grieving families.

At the end of our performance, we wrapped the audience in 10' x 10' banners the length of a football field made of thousands of paper hands—each one signed with a promise from someone who had seen our show in the Midwest, pledging to use their hands to help, not to harm.

Our Banners of Signed Hands - ARCh Youth Team 2002 in DC

I watched the crowd weep. Not because we were perfect performers. But because we made them *feel* something. Because we reminded them they weren't alone.

My eyes opened in that moment, and I understood what it meant to create impact. I started to believe...Maybe I wasn't meant to *just* exist. I was here to make a difference.

From Found to Lost in the Spotlight

I found purpose on those ARCh stages—dressed in makeshift costumes, performing skits about bullying and self-esteem for kids who reminded me of myself.

It was raw, real, and imperfect, but it mattered. I had a voice, a role I was proud of, and a reason to show up.

But the applause fades quickly when the curtain closes.

The truth is, I didn't know how to hold on to that version of me. I still lived in a world that valued appearance over authenticity and perfection over presence.

And as much as I wanted to stay grounded in that purpose-driven girl, the pull of validation was louder. Especially when it came wrapped in compliments and camera flashes.

It started small.

When I was 17, I was 'found' as a model. I signed with an agency and started booking photo shoots, runways, and commercials.

Honestly, it felt like a dream come true at first. Compliments, praise, and validation for how I looked. Exactly what I thought I needed. And definitely what I thought I wanted.

I was drawn into a world that was looking for someone unique to stand out amidst the cookie-cutter stand-ins of size 2 models. And I fit the mold—a curvy 'Marilyn Monroe' type with gorgeous in-your-face hair and a large smile - at least that's what the people who 'found' me said!

**Runway Modeling at the Start of My
Modeling Career - 2003**

My first time modeling for Redken 5th Avenue and Justin Isaac, I thought maybe this was the "more" I had been searching for. This was the way into the glamorous life the world was telling me I needed to strive for.

So I followed the light. But I didn't realize it until much later...sometimes the brightest spotlight casts the darkest shadow.

The modeling world promised significance, but it came with a cost. I was thrown into an industry where confidence was currency, and I was already in debt.

I didn't walk in with a strong sense of self. I walked in with questions, with cracks, with a quiet desperation to be wanted. And the industry didn't heal those things; it fed on them.

Suddenly, I wasn't the girl with a purpose—I was a product. And as the expectations grew louder, my voice got quieter. Until it almost disappeared entirely.

There were points in my modeling career where I stood in front of a mirror. Not to admire myself—but to dismantle myself.

I was taught that beauty was a goalpost, a costume. I was told if I could just shrink enough, smile enough, stay quiet enough...then maybe I'd be worthy of being seen.

This poem is about the price I paid for that visibility. The damage I endured in the name of being "perfect." The war waged on my body—and my identity—in an industry that applauds the image but silences the soul.

This isn't just my story. It's the story of millions of girls who traded pieces of themselves to become what someone else defined as beautiful.

I call this piece...

An Army of Broken Soldiers

You think I'm beautiful
And smart
Oh... not in that audition,
not playing that part

It's okay I understand
I've gotta change to have success
My hips are too big,
I'm way too emotional
You're right, I'm such a mess.

Let me twindle down to flesh & bones
Maybe then I'll be good enough
I'll change my face even...
Smooth, contour & pluck

Your brutal judgments & demeaning blows
They've all made me tough
This life is a career
I agree...you can't JUST be good enough

When I was growing up,
You defined the beauty ideal
I would stare & admire at what to me
Was unreal

Walking runway, being a model
Being displayed for all to see
I wanted that life so bad,
I could barely breathe

Now that I'm here, I get it
I'm here to be mocked at and torn apart
Being beautiful isn't valuable
It's just considered art

This is my job I suppose
Beauty is really only skin deep
You don't care about my personality
Being a model isn't cheap

In the end, I want to thank you
For making me look so good
In that show, in that photo shoot
You made me feel exactly how I knew you would
If only for one moment, it was all so clear
You dressed me, you shaped me
This is my modeling career

I've turned out exactly how you've wanted
Focused on flaws and my looks

No longer a mess on the outside
But inside - tortured, scared & mistook

But as long as I don't show it
And I continue to play the part
I'm still your prized possession
I'm still your...work of art

You win every time,
Every battle, every war
Where there once was one girl
Now lies a million more

You've built your army of broken soldiers
Hiding behind masks of beauty trends
No one fights you anymore,
Everyone just bends

So this is what it is to be a model
All eyes on me
I'm beautiful, I'm perfect
I'm where I always wanted to be

Our relationship has been rocky
But I hold no spite
Because who I once was
Can no longer put up a fight

Me Modeling Between 2002 (Top Left) and 2006 (Bottom)

When Magic Goes Silent

Let me tell you, you lose yourself and any sense of magic pretty quickly when you lose your fight.

After high school, I was scouted and signed by an international modeling agency. Within months, I was walking runways, wearing designer gowns, and boarding private jets. My name was on contracts, and my images were splashed across fashion spreads, storefronts, beauty ads, and billboards. People told me I had "made it."

But I was disappearing.

I stopped eating. Then I started binging and purging.

My hair thinned. My teeth yellowed. My joy evaporated. I was shrinking in more ways than one.

From the outside, it looked like I had it all—the career, the beauty, the success.

But on the inside, I was floundering. No one knew how much I was hurting, not even the people closest to me. I used that perfect smile to cover up all my pain.

And then came the night I broke.

I was 20 and I found myself in the fluorescent-lit bathroom of a 24-hour McDonald's in Phoenix, AZ, staring into a mirror that only reflected what I wanted to forget.

I was a skeleton of a girl with nothing left to prove...and no idea how to get out. The voices were screaming. The shame was deafening.

And then—just for a moment—I tried to make it stop. Hoping to drown the pain, the noise, the self-loathing, I attempted to take my own life.

It wasn't drama. It was desperation.

As I stood there in my tear-soaked shirt, mascara running down my cheeks, something inside me whispered...*stop*. I collapsed on the floor sobbing. And there, in the quiet, something stirred.

Not a miracle. Not a revelation. Just... stillness.

Looking back now, I know that was the first time I met my Witness—the calm, observing presence inside me that doesn't flinch in the face of chaos.

She didn't offer answers. She didn't rescue me. She just stayed and acknowledged the pain, the trauma, the suffering—all of it. And that... was enough.

The next morning, my mother came to rescue me. As we started the long drive from Arizona to Wisconsin, the failure I felt as a model began to sync in. And the fear about my future became almost unbearable.

Over the next year, I struggled with eating disorders and body dysmorphia while living back at my parent's home. I was overwhelmed by grief and loneliness, with no clarity of what came next.

For what felt like an eternity, I sat in the grief of losing my identity, trying to make sense of what modeling truly meant to me.

At first, all I could see was what I lost—the spotlight, the applause, the glam and glitz, the amazing wardrobe, the image.

But then, I remembered the magic!

How their vision of me as the next Marilyn Monroe helped me see that magic in myself. How the stage and the lights transcended me from a lost, lonely, awkward girl into a proud, strong woman on a runway.

I realized I was meant for more than being *just* a model.

I was made to be a **role** model. To challenge the norm. To stand as an example. To create a ripple in an industry that, at the time, left no room for difference.

So...I went back to work—but on my terms.

I modeled in my community without an agency. I walked runways at fashion weeks, appeared on billboards, and graced local magazine covers. I didn't just accept my 48-inch hips—I learned to love them.

And as I began to recognize my natural beauty, others did too.

For most of my twenties, I still approached mirrors with caution, uncertain of my relationship with the modeling world.

But finally, for the first time, I began to accept what I saw.

Modeling for Lyle Husar Designs in Wisconsin - 2006

Motherhood and the Mirror (Again)

Savannah and I - 2015

Years later, I would stand in front of another mirror—this time as a new mother, holding my six-week-old baby girl, Savannah.

She was perfect. Whole. Innocent. And I...was terrified. I had traded runway lights for the soft glow of a nursery. And once again, I found myself unraveling.

Postpartum depression didn't arrive with dramatic flair. It crept in quietly, like a fog curling around the edges of my joy, numbing me from the inside out. I believed being a mother meant sacrificing everything—my dreams, my identity, my desires.

So I did.

I let go of everything that made me feel like me. And soon I couldn't tell the difference between love and resentment. I was angry at my beautiful, precious, perfect baby for taking things I hadn't even realized I still wanted. And the shame of that nearly broke me.

I wore a beautiful mask—one of love, strength, warmth—but underneath, I was cracking beneath the weight of it all. I became detached. Numb. Hollow.

I saw it happening, but I couldn't stop it. The guilt of feeling unhappy in my new role as a mom was crushing. The shame was unbearable. And once again, I started to silently drown in the overwhelm.

But then came another mirror moment.

Savannah had just turned one. I was going through the motions of motherhood—smiling, posting photos, celebrating milestones. But when I looked at myself in the mirror, I barely recognized the woman looking back. She was exhausted, lost, a dulled version of her once radiant self.

A woman who had forgotten who she was.

But then... a flicker. Behind my tired eyes, I saw her. A younger version of me. The fifteen-year-old with a spark who once stood on the steps of the Capitol, believing she could change the world. The girl who lit up rooms—not because of how she looked—but because of who she was becoming.

I'm not sure what stirred it up exactly...maybe it was the stillness of that moment, or the weight of Savannah's future pressing gently against my own. Maybe it was the sheer contrast between who I had been and who I had become.

But something in me sparked.

A whisper. A remembering. A sacred ache to return to the girl who dreamed out loud, and to become the kind of woman that girl would one day be proud of. In that mirror moment, I made a life-altering decision.

If I wanted my daughter to grow up believing in herself, she needed to see her mom doing the same.

I realized in that moment that my perfect Savannah didn't take anything away from me—she gave me back to myself. She didn't replace my identity; she revealed it. She illuminated a pathway I had forgotten was mine—a way back to the parts of me I'd buried beneath survival, success, and self-sacrifice.

In her tiny hands, I saw the permission I hadn't known I was waiting for. To soften. To grow. To remember.

She wasn't *just* my daughter—she was my mirror, my muse, my reason to finally become the woman I was always meant to be.

And in that moment, she became my hero and my greatest teacher.

The Birth of Positive Presence

Within 90 days of that mirror moment, I launched what would become Positive Presence. I didn't know what it was yet, I just knew I had to create it. I didn't have a business plan. I didn't have a road map.

What I did have was a fire inside me—burning with equal parts fear and faith. I scribbled a thought I heard in my head like a prayer:

"Positivity can only spread when it is present."

At first, it seemed simple—something about confidence, optimism, and showing up with intention. I didn't know exactly what it would become. I just knew it had to start.

So I began where I felt most equipped to serve: coaching teen girls on modeling. It was the world I came from—the runway, the spotlight, the relentless pressure to perform. I knew the cracks in that world because I had fallen through them. I had the language, the experience, and the passion to help young girls navigate that space with more self-love and resilience than I ever had.

I thought I was teaching them how to walk and pose. But it quickly became clear: what they really needed wasn't instruction. It was permission.

What started as a vision rooted in modeling evolved into something much deeper. I wasn't just teaching girls how to carry themselves on the outside—I was helping them find a reason to stand tall on the inside. And that's when I realized... I wasn't building a business.

I was answering a calling.

But session after session, something started to shift. They didn't care about how to slay a photoshoot. They cared about how to stop hating their bodies. How to talk to their parents. How to be okay with the thoughts in their heads. How to trust their own voice. They were asking, silently and not-so-silently:

Am I enough? Am I lovable? Am I allowed to be who I am?

I knew those questions well. They didn't want a coach. They wanted a Witness. Someone who could sit with them in their fear and not flinch. Someone who has been where they've been and succeeded in getting to the other side.

So I threw out the scripts. I let go of the perfect image. I started telling them the truth about my battles—with food, with confidence, with shame, with motherhood, with my body, with my mind.

And then something miraculous happened.

When I shared my shadows, they shared theirs. They opened up. One by one, wall by wall, they let me in. And when they saw their truth reflected in my honesty... something unexplainable happened.

They started to heal. We weren't just building confidence. We were building a connection.

And that... was magic.

The Room Inside Me

As I continued this work with my students, something happened that would change how I saw myself forever.

One night, just past midnight, while my family was asleep, I sat in the quiet, calm hum of my home. I was sitting on the floor of my office, legs tucked under me, the dim glow of a salt lamp casting warm shadows on the walls. Outside, a soft snow had just begun to fall—slow, silent, peaceful.

I was emotionally drained that night, but spiritually open. I had just wrapped a week of coaching sessions that cut deep—stories of heartbreak, loneliness, and trying so hard to belong. Their pain felt eerily familiar and stirred something in me that I couldn't shake.

So I closed my eyes.

In the blurred white hue of my mind's eye, I envisioned myself standing in a room. The air felt heavy but safe, like a sanctuary made from memory.

As the fog settled, this internal version of me gazed around my sacred imagined space. I was surrounded by women and children - some young, some old and gray, some extremely confident, and some obviously breaking. Some were radiant, their energy crackling like lightning. Others were curled in the corners, grieving or afraid. Some stared ahead with boldness. Some wouldn't meet my gaze at all. I continued to look around at each of these women...and that's when I realized:

They were all me.

I observed all the versions of me in real time.

Each one was a role I'd played in life. Some were thriving. Some were sobbing. Some were frozen in fear.

The model—tired, desperate to be loved.
The mother—grieving her identity.
The CEO—fierce but terrified.
The teenager—angry and unsure.
The coach. The daughter. The partner.
The broken girl on the McDonald's floor.
The dreamer. The student.

They were all in that room. All alive within me.

And in the center... was this radiant beam of light. Less a person and more a personification of presence. She didn't need to say or do or be anything. She simply radiated.

That was my Witness.

The part of me that held me through every storm. The one who had never left.

Since then, I've come to believe we all carry a room like that inside us—populated by our inner archetypes (mom, sister, CEO, wife, visionary, etc.).

And when we begin to listen...to observe without judgment...we begin to heal. We don't need to become someone new. We need to embrace the many versions of ourselves that already exist—the bold, the broken, the becoming. Each one holds a piece of our truth.

And, together, with the Witness in the center, they form the whole. This kind of presence is always there, waiting for each of us to discover it within ourselves.

The Psychology of the Witness

In Buddhist teachings, what I refer to as the Witness is called the **inner observer**—the part of the self that exists beyond emotion, ego, or identity. In trauma therapy, it's often described as the **wise mind** or **compassionate self.**

My Witness has been with me all along. She sat with me in the bathroom stall. She stood beside me in the modeling industry. She wept with me during postpartum numbness. She built this company, this mission, this movement. And when it was time to rise, she didn't push—she opened the door and walked with me into my world of light.

Now, I Invite you to meet your Witness.

Inside each of us is a room filled with the many versions of who we've been.

The roles we've played.
The masks we've worn.
The emotions we've carried.

Every chapter, every archetype, every past self is still echoing in the walls of who we are. Together, they shape your Witness. The quiet, steady presence who has seen it all—and still believes in you. And when we stop running from the room... when we slow down and dare to look inside,

That's when we find magic. The kind that helps you remember who you are—even when the world, and even you, have forgotten.

Truth Not a Trick

Your magic lives in your presence. It's in your ability to stay with yourself, even when the road turns difficult. To hold your own hand. To whisper, "I love you," even when you falter. To witness your story fully, without abandoning the parts you long to forget.

You don't need to perform to be powerful. You don't need to be fixed to be worthy. You just need to begin listening. That is the first act of magic: to see yourself.

You are not a role to fill. You are a reckoning—a quiet fire. Proof that becoming yourself is the bravest thing you'll ever do.

Every hat I've ever worn—model, mother, CEO, failure, fighter—was never the whole picture. They were invitations. And each one asked me the same question:

Are you willing to see yourself not as one role, but as the beautiful sum of all your parts?

And now, I ask you the same. Because your story matters—not just the highlight reel—but the messy, mundane, painful, beautiful whole of it. Your magical abilities are not waiting for you at the end of a to-do list. They are already inside you, woven into your story, humming beneath your skin, just waiting for your permission to be seen.

So close your eyes. Call your Witness forward. And let that energy whisper what you already know:

You were never broken. You were just becoming.

Reflection Invitations

Throughout this book, you'll find gentle pauses—reflection invitations—placed at the end of each chapter. They aren't assignments or checklists. They're soul prompts. Little open doors that lead you back to yourself.

Each invitation offers space to breathe, to wonder, to reconnect. You don't need to answer them all. You don't have to answer them perfectly. You just need to let them land.

Some you might sit with in silence. Some you might write out in a journal. Some you might come back to months from now when the timing feels right. My hope is that these questions guide you into the parts of yourself you're ready to rediscover.

Let this be a conversation with your Witness, your inner wisdom, your light.

- What was your first spark - that moment you felt connected to something greater than yourself?

- Are there parts of your life you've tried to hide that might actually be your greatest source of wisdom?

- Who is in the room of your archetypes? Which ones need more attention, forgiveness, or love?

2

Your Lifespark

What drives you forward when everything feels impossible? What keeps you going when the obstacles feel insurmountable?

For me, the answer lies in something I call the **Lifespark.**

The Lifespark is an unshakable force that lives inside each of us. It's more than just a fleeting feeling or temporary goal. It is when you intentionally choose actions that reflect and express the most authentic, meaningful reasons you feel you are here, not just surface goals, habits, or to-do lists, but the core values or driving force within you.

It's about ensuring what you do in the world matches who you are at your most meaningful, purpose-driven level. When you discover your Lifespark, it's like tapping into an inner reservoir—one that continually replenishes you, nourishing your spirit even in life's most challenging moments.

Here's an important note: a Lifespark isn't quite the same as *purpose.*

Purpose is your why—your reason for moving through the world with intention. It's powerful. It matters. But your Lifespark is what fuels your purpose.

It's the divine current running underneath it all. It's what remains even when you question the path, doubt your calling, or feel like you've lost your way.

Where purpose can sometimes feel like something you need to define or chase, your Lifespark is something you already carry. You feel it. It pulls you. It hums beneath the surface until you're ready to remember it again.

Finding your Lifespark might start as a whisper or burst forth like a roar. A quiet flicker or a sudden blaze. It may not come with immediate clarity, but once it touches you, it leaves an undeniable imprint on your soul.

Your Lifespark is not just a calling. It's a **knowing**—a gravitational pull that guides you forward even when you want to collapse.

It's the invisible current that surges through your bloodstream when you've found your "why." The thing that makes you stand up when everything inside you wants to fold.

This chapter is about understanding the difference between purpose and a Lifespark, and why that distinction matters. Because when you know your Lifespark, you don't just walk toward your future...you ignite it.

And once you've touched it, once you've felt that divine alignment, you begin to trust the path ahead, even when life gets messy.

From Purpose to Lifespark

I used to think purpose was something you did. A job. A title. A plan with tidy milestones. But I've come to learn that purpose rarely shows up fully formed or neatly packaged. It arrives as a quiet invitation to begin. A whisper. A pull. That invisible voice inside that says, **"Keep going."**

Purpose is magnetic in a way that defies logic—you'd follow it even when the path feels impossible. Especially then.

I didn't start Positive Presence because I wanted clout or accolades. I started it because I believed—with every cell in my body—that every teenager deserves the opportunity to kindly discover themselves alongside a compassionate, trusted, non-judgmental role model.

At first, I thought I was just model coaching. That was the door I walked through—unaware that life was already steering me toward something much bigger. That was the invitation.

It wasn't until 2018, when I lost one of my former students, Marek, to suicide, that my quiet purpose ignited into something far greater. That was the moment my purpose became my **Lifespark.**

The heartbreak of Marek's death cracked me open in a way that made everything feel urgent, raw, honest, and non-negotiable. What had once been a quiet belief transformed into a blazing mission: **To eradicate teen suicide globally by 2035.**

THAT is my Lifespark. Not a title. Not a job. It began to fuel every decision I made. And that kind of clarity shifted my compass from fear to devotion. Eradicating teen suicide globally is not a slogan.

It's my soul's assignment, with a fast-approaching due date.

I've built an entire life around that mission—not because I knew how I'd do it, but because I couldn't live with myself if I didn't try. And that's how you know you've touched your Lifespark: When you're willing to risk rejection, discomfort, and security for something that feels bigger than you.

When the Spark Flickers

I've known my Lifespark since that heartbreaking day in May 2018 when we lost Marek, but one of the most soul-defining moments that challenged my devotion to it came in the form of a lease.

In August 2023, I signed the most terrifying and exhilarating contract of my life: a seven-year lease on Positive Presence's corporate headquarters. Over 2,200 square feet of vision, risk, and blind faith.

A half-million-dollar investment. It felt like a shiny new sanctuary for my dreams, just minutes from my home in downtown Chanhassen, MN.

I stood in the center of that empty space after the glasses clinked and the papers were signed, keys in hand…heart pounding. Sunlight streamed through the windows like a wink from the Universe—as if it knew something I hadn't yet accepted: I was stepping into a destiny I'd been preparing for all along (even if I couldn't quite see it yet myself).

**Me With My Key to My New
Corporate Headquarters**

The feeling reminded me of the day I found out I was having a daughter—beaming on the outside, but quietly trembling on the inside. Only this time, instead of fear paralyzing me, I let the pounding in my chest feel like a drumbeat—one guiding me toward something bold and sacred.

This space wasn't just an office. It was the foundation for a dream I had nurtured for years—creating local, in-person life coaching centers for teens across the country.

Positive Presence had evolved far beyond its early days of model coaching. It had grown into a national life-coaching movement offering virtual mentorship to teens and young adults all over the world. We built a powerful virtual coaching experience rooted in emotional intelligence, personal growth, and deep, trusted connection.

But post-COVID, our clients were hungry for more than virtual connections and conversations—they longed for human interaction. For a physical space where they could be comfortable while they practice confidence, be supported while they spoke about their challenges, and feel safe even if they're not sure what they're running from.

When I held the key in my hand, I didn't just unlock a door. I unlocked a new version of myself. It was the tangible amalgamation of my Lifespark.

It was about planting something real into the earth, declaring to the universe—and to myself—**that I was all in.**

But just because you've found your Lifespark doesn't mean it's always clear. Sometimes, it fades into the background—buried beneath the noise of disappointment, doubt, and discouragement. Or deafened by life's constant distractions.

Just nine months after that champagne toast, I found myself on the same floor, sobbing.

Despite countless community meetings, proposals, and conversations with city officials, educators, and business leaders, I couldn't gain traction. The doors I thought would fly open stayed bolted shut. I was ghosted. Dismissed. Patronized.

One school board member even told me I was "too pedigreed to be relatable." No matter what I did, I kept hearing **"no."** I felt paralyzed. As if I had climbed halfway up the mountain, only to look up and realize I'd somehow slid all the way back to the base.

I had spent years traveling the country, changing lives with Positive Presence—yet in my own hometown, I was being patted on the head. Rebuffed by people who didn't care to understand what we did.

My spark began to flicker.

I questioned everything—my purpose, my decisions, my worth. Gasping for air, I called my landlord and begged to get out of the lease, but he wouldn't let me. I felt like my dream had become a burden, and everything connected to it became an unbearable weight I carried on my shoulders.

That's what loss feels like. I felt confusion. Humiliation. Doubt. Rage. A disappointment so tangled I couldn't breathe through it. I was still smiling during sessions for my virtual students and team, but inside, I was crumbling, quietly drowning in rejection. It was one of the loneliest, most sobering seasons of my life.

The Psychology of Purpose

Here's something I've come to understand—not just from experience, but from research:

Purpose is one of the most powerful protectors of mental health.

It gives struggle meaning. It turns pain into progress. It anchors us when we feel adrift. Psychologist Dr. William Damon defines purpose as:

"A stable and generalized intention to accomplish something that is at once meaningful to the self and consequential to the world."

In other words, purpose turns heartbreak into a blueprint. And that's what happened next for me. Because after months in the dark, feeling defeated and lost, that familiar hum inside me began to rise again. My Lifespark hadn't abandoned me. It simply waited for me to realign.

That's the truth about a Lifespark: It never dies. It flickers. It fades. But it waits—patiently, powerfully—until you're ready to reach for it again.

And I did.

I stopped chasing the approval of people who didn't get it. And I redirected my energy toward the people who did. I refined the pitch. Rewrote the strategy. Realigned with the heartbeat of the work.

To eradicate teen suicide globally by 2035.

The "no's" didn't disappear. But I wasn't devastated by them anymore. I saw beyond them. What I gained from that experience was even more resilience than I thought I had.

I learned to hear the criticism, the rejection, the negativity, and rise above it. I found an appreciation for the no's because they helped me grow stronger.

It was a realignment - an opportunity to choose the right path for ME. That's what a Lifespark offers, it doesn't shield you from pain, but it helps you carry it.

It doesn't make you invincible, but it makes you unshakable.

The Slingshot Effect

It's easy to think of a Lifespark as something we go out and find, like treasure buried just beneath the surface of our circumstances.

But more often, it's something that finds us—when we stop pretending, start listening, and choose to live with honesty.

That's when the Witness within us awakens. The part of us that doesn't flinch, judge, or force, but simply sees.

And when we let Witness lead, even the setbacks become sacred.

For me, that sacred spark didn't arrive with fanfare. It didn't explode like lightning. It rose quietly, like the sun, warm and steady. And it rose, unmistakably, in the faces of the teens and young adults I've coached over the years.

Each story. Each struggle. Each hallowed "aha." They weren't just students. They were soul-mirrors. They reminded me that the core of my Lifespark isn't rooted in ambition—it's rooted in empathy. In sitting with someone's pain and refusing to let them face it alone.

That's my magic. The magic that fuels my purpose. The purpose that revealed my Lifespark.

But here's the truth no one talks about:

Even when you know your Lifespark—even when you're living it—there are still moments when the path disappears beneath your feet. Moments when the momentum slows, the vision clouds, and progress stalls. Moments when the doubt screams louder than your purpose ever could.

That happened to me after I opened the doors to the Positive Presence HQ. What should have been a triumphant season turned into a season of silence. Rejection. Ghosting. Red tape. Misunderstanding. Defeat.

It felt like I was climbing uphill with bricks tied to my ankles—like no one could see the dream I was carrying, and worse, no one cared to.

I questioned everything. My timing. My leadership. My ability to carry this mission forward. That was my slingshot moment. But I didn't know it at the time. It wasn't until I paused and asked myself,

"What if this isn't a setback? What if this is a setup?"

What if life was pulling me back, not to break me, but to build the tension, the pressure, the *momentum* I needed to launch forward with more clarity, strength, and conviction than ever before?

That's what many people in the personal and professional development space call the **Slingshot Effect.**

It's the divine pullback that feels like failure—when nothing seems to work, when progress disappears, and when your belief in yourself wavers.

But the slingshot doesn't fire without resistance. It doesn't fly until it's pulled back far enough to gather force. And when it releases? The flight is fast, focused, and fearless.

Once I leaned into my slingshot, Positive Presence began to grow again, not just in size, but in soul. We expanded across the country tenfold, amplified our global impact, and became a lifeline for students and families seeking more than just inspiration—they needed real, actionable impact.

My leadership team and I became stronger and more connected as we expanded our mentor-coaching team from ten to twenty, then to sixty, and beyond. Each step brought us closer to our mission: to eradicate teen suicide, not only by saving lives, but by equipping the next generation to save themselves, and each other.

That's what the slingshot taught me: Just because you feel pulled back doesn't mean you're falling behind. It may be the tension that precedes your most meaningful launch.

So if you're in that pullback right now...hold steady. You are not being punished. You are being *positioned.*

Your Lifespark isn't just the thing that ignites a fire amidst the darkest moments in your life, it's the rhythm—the breath. The forward motion you keep choosing – day after day – as you grow into the person and the presence you were always meant to be.

Not a destination. But a direction. Not a single moment. But a sacred momentum. And when it lifts you, you'll know:

This is what the waiting was for.

Your Lifespark is Waiting

If you're still searching for your Lifespark, know this: It's not lost. It's not hiding from you. It's already within you, waiting to be noticed.

Your Lifespark doesn't always arrive with clarity. It reveals itself in alignment. It shows up in the moments when you feel most like you. When something inside you says, *this matters*—even when it's hard.

You'll catch glimpses of it in the things that tug at your heart. In the dreams you can't shake. In the causes, the people, the ideas that stir something ancient in your soul. The moments when your body exhales and your spirit rises.

You'll stumble. You'll doubt. You'll hit walls that make you question everything. That's okay. The spark doesn't disappear—it waits.

It flickers through resistance. It hums beneath the fear. It stays lit, quietly urging you forward, step by brave step. And one day, without even realizing it, you'll look up and see:

You're no longer just seeking your Lifespark. You're living it. Not perfectly. Not all at once. But intentionally. Beautifully. Aligned. That's how you know the fire is real. And that it's yours.

Reflection Invitations

- Have you ever felt something inside you that felt bigger than your current life? What would it look like to follow that spark?

- Think of a time when your purpose felt out of reach. What did that experience reveal about what you truly value?

- Who have you supported or witnessed through struggle? What did that teach you about your purpose?

- What does your ideal life look like—not just in success, but in spirit?

- What would it feel like to live in full alignment with your Lifespark?

- When have you experienced one of the signs that you've touched your spark? What might it be pointing you toward?

3

Facing Your Fears

Fear doesn't always crash through the door. Sometimes, it just stands in the corner - quiet, watching, waiting, whispering.

For most of my life, fear has shown up like a cold hand under still water, reaching for my ankle. Pulling, tightening. And before I know it, I'm gasping - caught in a current I didn't even know was there.

Fear, for me, has never been just an emotion. It's a shapeshifter. A shadow. A presence. It follows me down hallways, hides behind doors, lingers even in joy—waiting to remind me it still has a grip.

Sometimes I dance with it. Sometimes I run from it. Sometimes I collapse and let its cold grip hold me. But here's what I've learned: the only way through fear...is with it.

Fear only visits those who are on the brink of growth. It is the final gate before expansion. The reverent tension before transformation. Fear, I've come to believe, isn't here to stop us. It's here to ask:

Are you ready to meet yourself, even here?

When Fear Wore a Pink Bow

The first time I truly recognized fear—not just felt it, but looked it in the eye—was the day I found out I was having a baby girl. I had convinced myself it was a boy. I felt it in my bones.

So when the doctor smiled and said, "It's a girl!", everyone around me cheered. And while I smiled, too...something inside me broke open—a silent, shapeless panic.

In the days that followed, I tried to talk myself into joy. Bows. Braids. Mother-daughter moments. I told myself how lucky I was. But the smile never quite reached my eyes.

Until one afternoon, alone in my room, surrounded by baby clothes, I collapsed. Tears spilled from a place so deep I didn't even recognize it. My heart raced. My hands trembled. I couldn't breathe.

Not because I didn't want a daughter. But because I didn't know how to protect her from the world that had hurt me.

How could I raise a girl in a world that had brutalized, betrayed, and broken so many women, including me?

That's when I realized something truly groundbreaking: I wasn't afraid *for* her. I was afraid *because* of her. Because her very existence asked me to finally face what I hadn't yet healed in myself.

That's when fear stopped being the villain—and instead became the child inside me, needing love, not judgment. And I became the parent—steady, compassionate, finally ready to hold what had always been mine to heal.

I had to learn to parent the little girl within me...before I could fully show up for the baby girl I was about to hold in my arms..

Some fears don't shout—they whisper. They sit quietly in the corner of our minds, disguised as logic, dressed as protection, dancing with us in silence. Healing isn't always linear, and sometimes the deeper we go, the louder the shame becomes.

This poem came from one of those moments—when I thought I had healed only to find an old wound still bleeding beneath the surface.

It's about the back-and-forth, the wanting and resisting, the aching to move forward while something invisible holds you in place.

This is a confession. A reckoning. A quiet plea for peace.

I call it **"The Fear Tango."** Because some of our deepest growth doesn't come from fighting fear—but from learning how to dance with it.

There is this darkness deep inside of me
That I used to be trapped in
Even though it has shrunk in size,
It still feels like I'm being held captive

A wound so deep it can't be healed
A hole too big to fill
A sinking ship lost at sea
A feeling of hopelessness I just can't kill

It pulls me when I want to be set free
It laughs at me when I try to be understood
It bullies me when I want to be its friend
And it makes me feel like I can't...
...even though I think I could

I could let it go and heal this wound
I could appreciate the contrast it so
effortlessly preserves
I could dive deeper with someone who cares
Or...
I could find the inner peace I so desperately deserve

I want to fully step into tomorrow
proud of my strength and grace
But I can't, and I won't move forward

Because no amount of healing can
cover the shame on my face.

The Dance Continues

As the late Vietnamese Zen master, poet, and peace activist
Thich Nhat Hanh once wrote:

*"The first part of looking at our fear is just inviting it into our aware-
ness without judgment. Then, once our fear has calmed down, we can
embrace it tenderly and look deeply into its roots."*

Although I didn't know anything about Hanh and his brilliance
at the time, in that moment on the floor of my unborn daughter's room, my Witness, unbeknownst to me, guided me to do
exactly that.

And it's something I continue to practice even now.

Because fear doesn't leave. It returns when we level up. When
we break old patterns. When we step into the unknown. But
now, when it returns, I don't see it as a threat. I see it as a
threshold.

In those moments as a new mother, fear didn't leave me, it re-
treated to a quieter place within me.

But that's the thing about fear – it quells in one area and swells
in another. Though my fear of raising a daughter had subsided,
my fear as a leader and entrepreneur exploded.

Every time I faced this new, visceral kind of fear, it felt like it reached for me with an outstretched hand, pulling me into a dance I didn't know the steps to.

It led, and I followed, pushed, and pulled like a reluctant partner, captive to its rhythm. I became entranced and entrenched in the feeling of fear; I couldn't escape it. It took over every part of me until I couldn't tell the difference between the voice of fear and my voice of reason.

I call it **the fear tango**...Fear grips my hand, tight, commanding. And I follow, inexplicably but gracefully.

I became such a good dancer. To the world, I was thriving—running a company, raising a family, giving talks and making moves. But inside? I was spinning. Tight-chested. Sweaty-palmed. Second-guessing everything. Ashamed by what I was feeling deep within.

The truth is, growth doesn't quiet fear—it invites more of it.

Because the more you expand, the more there is at stake. You fear failure. You fear success. You fear disappointing your team, your family, your dreams. You fear finally being seen—and not being enough once you are.

I've stood on stages. Sat in boardrooms as the only woman. Pitched my vision to leaders who smiled, nodded—and disappeared. Held back tears outside the Positive Presence HQ when no one showed up. And still, I showed up. With a shaky voice. With imposter syndrome. With exhaustion.

Because I've learned: Even when fear takes the lead, I can choose to keep dancing. Not to win. Not to conquer. But to honor the movement, and keep going.

But here's one thing to consider...sometimes, the dance becomes heavier than we expect—less like a performance, more like a pilgrimage. There are seasons when fear doesn't just visit your mind—it finds its way into your bones and settles there.

For me, one of those seasons began in 2021—on a long stretch of highway, toward a man who had shaped much of my fear, and unknowingly held the key to releasing it.

From Powerlessness to Peace

In November 2021, I found myself making the same 3½-hour drive to my parents' house in Wisconsin again and again, overwhelmed by the fear of losing my father.

My dad has survived lung cancer at the peak of COVID and had gotten into remission, but right around Thanksgiving, he relapsed, and something felt off.

His breathing was labored. His body was worn down. And deep in my bones, I knew—this time was different.

He had been fighting for years. After decades spent smoking, drinking, and working in unforgiving conditions—he became diagnosed with COPD.

For 23 years, he had served as a Boiler Technician and Oil King in the United States Navy—one of the most brutal and toxic environments aboard a ship.

Later, he became a nationally acclaimed Pump Technician, working with the same grit and sacrifice that defined much of his life. His lungs bore the weight of decades of devotion to service, to providing, to survival. Then came the cancer.

Through the COVID pandemic, he fought cancer with rounds of chemo and radiation, never complaining, always just...enduring. That was his way. Silent. Strong. Stubborn.

Growing up, we didn't talk about feelings in my family, especially not with my dad. He was a provider, a protector—but emotionally distant, weathered by trauma he rarely named and barely acknowledged.

Our relationship had been more scar than softness. And for most of my life, I unknowingly carried that silence like a wound. When I longed for closeness, I got correction. When I pursued my dreams, he called me foolish.

And now, as I drove those long stretches of highway in the brutal cold of a Midwest winter, I was grieving the loss of a kind, accepting version of him I thought I'd still have time to meet.

What I didn't know was this was the beginning of our healing—and the end of his life.

During those drives, I turned to a tool I teach my students: the Emotional Guidance Scale by Abraham Hicks. A ladder of emotional states—each one a step closer to joy and positivity.

I started in powerlessness. Whispered to shame. Screamed at guilt. Cursed regret. Then slowly climbed to anger. Bargained with overwhelm. Flirted with Frustration.

Until, mile by mile, I arrived at hope. I spoke aloud to willingness. I cried with understanding.

Eventually, I stopped trying to rewrite our history, and just began to love him as he was—a sort of acceptance I never thought I would be able to achieve in relationship to my father.

By my third drive, I saw him not as the father I *wanted*, but the man he *was*. And something inside me softened. By the time hospice was called, I began to love my father again. And more than that, I had made my way up the scale to something I never thought I'd reach with him: peace.

The Emotional Scale
Amalgamated from the work of Abraham Hicks & David R. Hawkins

POSITIVE
Enlightenment
Peace & Serenity
Joy
Love & Passion
Eagerness & Enthusiasm
Optimism

Acceptance & Harmony
Reason & Understanding
Willingness
Hope
Trust
Courage

Neutrality
Pride
Boredom

Worry
Disappointment
Impatience, Frustration, & Irritation
Overwhelmed
Scorn
Anger, Hate & Revenge
Jealousy
Insecurity & Unworthiness
Fear

Regret
Grief & Despair
Depression
Apathy
Guilt & Blame
Shame & Humiliation
Powerlessness
NEGATIVE

In his final days, I held his hand. I laid on his chest. I told him I was proud of all he's accomplished. And he said, for what seemed like the first time, "I love you. I'm proud of you." It didn't erase everything. But it helped me make new meaning out of our relationship.

His passing wasn't just the end of his life—it was the beginning of a new chapter in mine. A chapter where I began to view emotions not as enemies to conquer, but as messengers to listen to. And slowly, I learned the greatest lesson of all:

Healing isn't about controlling the path. It's about staying rooted in yourself as you walk it.

Becoming the Witness

There's a metaphor I use with my students: Life is like a roller coaster.

Most of us are strapped in, white-knuckled, bracing for the next drop. We feel every twist, every jolt, every rise and fall. But what if you could step off the ride? What if you stopped *being* swept away by the experience... and started *witnessing* it?

As the Witness, you're no longer the rag doll in the storm. You become the stillness at its center. You observe with compassion and clarity.

You stop asking, "Why is this happening to me?" And start wondering, "What is this here to show me?"

That shift changes everything. The chaos might still swirl—but your relationship to it transforms. The Witness doesn't resist. It doesn't control. It sits beside you, steady, open-hearted, unafraid of the mess. It doesn't rush you toward an answer. It simply stays.

And when you learn to live from that place—when you embody a quiet knowing—fear begins to loosen its grip. Because you're no longer ruled by the moment. You're anchored in meaning. You can hold the lesson behind the pain. Feel the emotion without becoming it.

You stop shrinking for the world, and begin expanding into your truth.

This is what it means to belong to yourself. To create internal spaciousness. To let fear visit, but never settle in. To become your own safe place.

You are not the roller coaster. You are the Witness. The breath between the drops. The calm, beneath the noise. The stillness that says:

"This too is part of me...and I am still whole."

You are the steady. You are the soul. You are the presence.

And that...is where your magic lives.

The Magic of Moving Through Fear

Fear has a way of making us feel paralyzed in singularity. The world becomes black and white. But when we learn to step outside of the fear and see the world for what it is—beautiful, colorful, multi-faceted, you will learn that:

You can feel everything, and still be steady. You can be afraid, and still move forward. You can be cracked open, and still be whole. You can be grieving, and still choose love.

You don't have to leap from darkness to light. From sad to happy. From fear to contentment, just take the next emotional rung.

That's the alchemy. That's the magic. That's where your power lives—not in pretending you aren't afraid, but in loving yourself through it.

You are not here to bypass your fear. You are here to befriend it and dance with it. And in doing so, you will meet yourself in the places that matter most.

Reflection Invitations

- Where in your life are you still gripping the safety bar, waiting for the drop?

- What would shift if you allowed yourself to observe your fear instead of becoming it?

- What's one emotion you can move toward today, even if just a little?

- What part of you still needs your presence—not your fixing?

- If fear wasn't something to fight but something to understand, what would it be trying to teach you?

4

The Power of Love

There are certain chapters in our lives where we don't even know we're lost—until someone shows us what it feels like to be found.

Between the ages of ten and twenty-four, I was lost in ways I didn't yet have language for. I felt like a phantom—wandering through the fog of girlhood into womanhood, unsure of who I was, who I wanted to be, or even what it meant to be "okay."

After my father retired from the Navy, we planted roots in Wisconsin—but that stability was more geographical than emotional.

He was entering a long, silent descent into PTSD and alcoholism, and my mom was essentially raising two kids (my brother and me) on her own, holding our household together with nothing but grit and sheer will.

I became the troublemaker—the girl who tested every boundary and broke rules before she even knew what the rules were. I talked back. I skipped class. I snuck out. I lied without flinching, pushed limits without hesitation. Not because I was brave or rebellious, but because it gave me the illusion of control.

I wasn't running toward anything. I was just running. Always. From what? I wasn't sure. Maybe from the weight of my dad's silence. Maybe from the tension that hung in our home like a heavy curtain we were all too afraid to pull back. Maybe from the ache of never really feeling seen—not for who I was, but for who I was becoming.

And staying still? Staying still meant feeling it. All of it. It meant facing a sadness that felt too big for my body to hold. It meant confronting the truth I didn't yet have the words for: That something inside me was already beginning to unravel.

So I kept moving. I filled my life with noise.
With drama.
With distractions.
Parties, boys, attention—anything that would numb the stillness, that would keep the quiet at bay.

I confused chaos for confidence. I wore my pain like armor and called it independence. But even the loudest distractions can't silence longing. And what I longed for most was to feel chosen. Wanted. Worthy.

That's when I started looking for love. Or at least... what I thought was love.

Every relationship in those years felt like a carnival game. The shiny ring toss or the oversized mallet and bell. The ones that seem so winnable. You spend your dollars, try your hardest, come so close, and lose every time.

But something in you believes that if you just try one more time, put in one more dollar, make one more effort, it'll all work out. You'll finally win the prize.

That was me. Over and over.

Trying to earn something that looked like love but was built on conditions, chaos, and confusion. High highs. Low lows. And in the lows—some of them deeply abusive—I kept chasing the hope of the next high. As if love had to be won, rather than simply received.

I didn't know then what I know now: Love isn't a prize you win. It's a presence you grow. But back then, I kept playing the game. And at one point, I thought I'd finally won.

In my early twenties I was engaged to a model—a man who embodied everything I thought I wanted. He was ripped, hardworking, the classic bad boy with just enough charm to make the turmoil seem worth it.

But the truth I couldn't yet admit to myself was that I wasn't drawn to him because he made me feel safe—I was drawn to him because he mirrored the parts of me that were still hurting.

We were fire and ice.

Explosive passion, volatile arguments, grand romantic gestures, followed by silent treatments that lasted days. There was no medium. No neutrality. Just a constant push and pull between desperation and desire.

He prided himself on his looks, mistaking charm for character. And I, still reeling from my own sense of failure after leaving the runway, clung to him like a lifeline.

But it wasn't love. It was attachment masquerading as intimacy. Validation disguised as connection.

And just like those carnival games, this too ended with me empty-handed. Another dollar down. Another lesson learned.

Another reminder that real love doesn't leave you guessing. Real love feels like safety, not suspense.

That relationship didn't just end. It unraveled me. But it also woke me up. Because once you've been burned by something that pretends to be love...you start to see things more clearly.

You learn the difference between chemistry and chaos. Between attention and affection. Between being chosen and being consumed.

And then, like a breath you didn't know you were holding, the right kind of love arrives. Not with fireworks. But with stillness.

When Love Finds You

Meeting Adam was like surfacing after years underwater.

We crossed paths in Lake Geneva, Wisconsin, on a quiet, unassuming afternoon that didn't yet know it would change everything. He had just left behind his nightlife career in Chicago to open a breakfast restaurant called Simple Cafe in this slow-moving lake town.

I was writing fashion and philanthropy columns for a new lifestyle paper (The Geneva Lakefronter), and found myself visiting this charming tourist town almost every weekend for events and inspiration.

It was the beginning of June 2010, and I walked into this historic home turned lounge club right across the lake, The Baker House. It became my go-to pre-bar to start all of my weekends off right. I was dating the bartender at the time—barely—but when he introduced me to Adam, something in me paused. Adam stood up tall, steady, and warm—the kind of presence that doesn't ask for attention, but naturally draws it in.

He handed me his card with a simple invitation: *"Next time you're in town, I'll buy you breakfast."* The card read: General Manager, Simple Cafe.

A few weekends passed, and then one night, the story began to write itself.

Another weekend, another gala. By then, my new Lake Geneva routine included texting Adam—and my old bartender fling-turned-friend—whenever I was heading into town. Most of the time, I'd find them both at The Baker House, drinks in hand.

Naturally, I would join them.

But one evening, I skipped the elegant gala altogether, accepting the consequences of a lost story for the magazine, and stayed with Adam for hours. We lost track of time, ordering food, sharing drinks as the world around us faded.

It felt like we'd known each other for years. Just conversation, laughter, and something soft, familiar, and unexpected unfolding between us.

When the night quieted, we wandered to the lakefront. The pier gate, usually locked, hung slightly open. We slipped through.

We saw the row of tour boats, usually wrapped and secured, and noticed one was uncovered. We stepped aboard.

Adam pulled a chair out for me, saw a crack in it, and replaced it with another chair. He took the broken one for himself and fell straight through it. We laughed until we cried.

Just as we heard footsteps—security doing rounds—we hid behind a cooler, usually empty, but today it was randomly fully stocked with ice and beer. It was like the Universe was conspiring in our favor!

He grabbed two and stuffed two more in his coat as we ducked, then ran to the nearby lifeguard tower to hide, both laughing historically like two kids on their personal playground.

The guard caught us, smiled, allowed us to stay, but took the open beers. We nodded, obedient. As soon as he left, Adam pulled the other two beers from his pocket. He opened one for me, one for himself.

And there, high above the sand, wind in our hair, like those beers, our hearts were cracked open by something honest and unexpected—we shared our first kiss.

That night wasn't planned. It wasn't polished. But it was real. The kind of love you don't earn or chase. The kind you just...meet.

Since Adam walked into my life in 2010, I have never once questioned his love or respect for me. That is a sentence I write with reverence. Not because our life has been easy, but because our love has been true.

Adam & I in 2010 (Left) and 2025 (Right)

Love didn't save me. It found me. And for the first time, I saw: Love was never something I had to earn. It took being truly loved by someone else to begin to see that.

And even still, I had work to do.

Our Blueprint

As Adam and I settled into our life together, we built something quiet but foundational—a compass that continues to guide us and our daughter, Savannah. At the center of that compass is one constant: **respect.**

It's our true north. It shapes how we speak to each other, how we present ourselves, and how we interact with and navigate the world as a family. Because when love is rooted in mutual respect, it can hold steady through anything. And it has.

Savannah, Adam & I (NYE 2024)

We don't avoid hard conversations. We don't bubble-wrap pain or gloss over the messy parts. We face them together. That, to me, is the quiet heroism of love.

It's not always fireworks or grand gestures. Sometimes, it's a steady hand during a hard moment. A truth spoken with care. A dance party in the kitchen on a Tuesday night when everything else in the world feels heavy.

That's what I now understand as true love.

Not perfect. Not easy. But present. Founded. Unshakably alive.

The Science Behind the Safety

There's something beautiful about realizing that what you feel in love isn't just emotional—it's physiological.

According to the Polyvagal Theory, when we feel emotionally safe in our relationships, our nervous system shifts into a ventral vagal state, characterized by calmness, regulation, and openness. This is why love can literally slow your heartbeat.

It's why your breath deepens in the arms of someone you trust. It's why we long to be seen, not just to be understood, but to feel safe enough to be ourselves.

Love that nurtures this kind of safety—be it romantic, parental, or platonic—*heals* us. It rewires what trauma and conditioning once taught us.

It teaches us that closeness isn't dangerous. That tenderness isn't weakness. That we can be loved without performing for it.

Oxytocin, often called the "love hormone," is released during physical affection, but also during emotional intimacy. Shared experiences. Eye contact. Laughter. Crying together. All of it feeds our inner sense of connection.

And connection, when real, creates capacity—For healing. For growth. For peace.

I remember one night, in the thick of my postpartum haze, I broke. Completely. I sat on the floor of our bathroom, knees pulled into my chest, sobbing in a way I hadn't let myself in years. I had no words—just tears.

And Adam didn't try to fix me. He didn't give me a speech or offer solutions. He just knelt beside me. Wrapped his arms around me. And breathed with me.

It was at that moment that I realized: *this* is what safety feels like. I felt like I was finally allowed to rest. I didn't need to be anything but human. I didn't need to be strong or successful or smiling.

I could just *be*. And he would stay.

That's when I learned the real magic of love—it's not in the grand gestures. It's in the quiet witnessing. The kind that says:

I'm here. You're safe. You don't have to carry this alone.

Self Love

But here's the truth I didn't understand in those early years of marriage and motherhood:

You can be deeply loved by others and still feel unworthy. Still feel hollow. Still be hiding from yourself. I had to learn, sometimes painfully, that other people's love wasn't a substitute for my own.

I had spent so many years chasing external validation—through relationships, through success, through perfection. I was always looking for someone or something to tell me I was enough because I didn't believe it on my own.

Even when I was being praised, I questioned if I deserved it. I hadn't yet learned the difference between being loved by others and believing I was worthy of love myself.

So I wore the masks. I stayed busy. I poured into others, hoping that if I could make them feel worthy, some of that worth would reflect back onto me.

But the truth I couldn't outrun was this: **I can't teach my students to love themselves if I don't know how to love myself.**

The love I offer others is only as strong as the love I allow for myself.

And so I began the work, not just of surviving or striving, but of softening.

Of listening.
Of choosing myself, again and again.

Self-love is the fierce decision to be your own lighthouse. To recognize when you are lost and guide yourself home. Again. And again. And again.

Even in the darkest of nights, and especially in the most tumultuous of storms.

The more I practiced being my own light and loving myself, the more I noticed something magical:

The love I gave others deepened because the love I gave myself was real.

We learn how to love ourselves not in isolation, but in reflection—From being seen, held, chosen, and respected. We borrow belief in our worth from those who see it first. And in time, we begin to believe it, too.

Let Love Be the Light

Remember this: Love doesn't save us. It reminds us.

That we are whole. That we are worthy. That even in the depths of our darkest moments, we are never beyond the reach of the light. And when we start to believe that...that's when we begin to rise.

So may you welcome the love that finds you. May you cherish the love that steadies you. And may you nurture the love within you—The kind that doesn't ask for proof. The kind that says: You are already enough. You are already home.

Let love be your lighthouse. Let it be your mirror. Let it be your magic.

And let it lead you all the way back to yourself.

Reflection Invitations

- Can you name a moment when you confused chaos for love? What did it teach you?

- Who in your life has shown you love in a way that made you feel safe?

- What does your inner compass say when you're over-whelmed?

- What is your version of respect?

- Can you feel the difference between being loved by someone else and loving yourself?

- If you were your own lighthouse, how can you guide yourself back to self love?

5

The Turning Point

There are moments when life asks you to move but gives you no map. Moments when everything you've built, everything you've believed, suddenly feels fragile. Far away. Fading.

Adam, Savannah, and I arrived in Minnesota in the dead of winter, January 2020, relocating, reorganizing, and re-acclimating our whole life.

I was carrying the weight of a business that felt like it was losing its pulse. Positive Presence had grown quiet amidst the chaos of this transition. Too quiet.

I had no team, only a few clients, and no idea of how I was going to transition a once-thriving business to a new region.

And for the first time in a long time, I wondered if maybe...I'd already lived the best parts of my dream.

We moved from Colorado to Minnesota for Adam's new job. It was an opportunity we both believed in. But when I arrived in this unfamiliar city with no connections, no community, and no knowledge of what I was going to do next, something inside me went still. I felt like a guest in my own life.

And then COVID hit.

The Breaking Point

I remember sitting in the kitchen of our new home one evening, surrounded by unopened boxes and unopened ideas, wondering if this was the end. Not the dramatic, cliffhanger kind of end. The slow kind. The kind that doesn't crash—it erodes.

One un-returned email. One declined payment. One more Colorado client who didn't want to continue virtual sessions. I remember staring at my bank account, hitting refresh like it might suddenly refill.

I wasn't just watching numbers, I was watching a dream slip away. Wondering if the world had already moved on from something I had poured my whole heart into.

I started browsing job boards. I updated my resume. I cried in the shower so my daughter wouldn't hear me breaking. But in the collapse, just as everything was falling to pieces around me, something remained...

It wasn't confidence. It wasn't clarity. It was something older. Something deeper. It was my *Lifespark*—the whisper of purpose that refuses to die.

Desperate to save my floundering business, I turned to Google and typed in: *web rep*. That's when I found MyWebReps.com, and Dan Murray. A stranger at the time, he would soon become a trusted mentor, a brilliant strategist, and my business's unexpected hero.

He didn't just take my call, he listened—really listened. And then, with quiet confidence, he laid out a simple plan he believed in deeply: one landing page and a $500 Google ad campaign. It wasn't flashy. It wasn't complicated. But it felt like hope. I maxed out a credit card and told myself—*this is the last try*. And I meant it.

And just like that, the air shifted. Not overnight. Not with fireworks. But subtly, like the first warm breeze from a long-awaited spring.

It started with one new client. Then another. Soon, it was five...then twenty. The momentum built quietly, organically. Word spread, not in headlines, but in hushed hope. People were still hurting. Still searching.

And while I was questioning my purpose, these strangers—from all corners of the country—were gently reminding me of it.

Suddenly, I felt reignited. I remembered my Lifespark. Maybe, just maybe, this wasn't the end after all.

I poured myself into the work. Long nights turned into all-nighters. Seventy-hour weeks stretched into eighty, then a hundred.

I was buzzing—like something inside me had re-awakened, spilling out in every direction. My body moved like a machine, driven by purpose.

I rebuilt our certification program from the ground up—infusing it with everything I'd learned and everything I still dreamed of teaching. I hired my first eight coaches (some former students) to test my certification program and affirm the model.

Dan and I met daily to strategize new methods and sharpen our messaging. I dared to dream bigger than ever before. And then...I looked back and realized all I had accomplished.

Within one year, Positive Presence grew by 120% year over year, followed by an additional 500% growth over the next year. We went from eight coaches to forty seemingly overnight. We were bursting at the seams—building, growing, evolving in every way imaginable.

Suddenly, I wasn't chasing clients—they were finding us. Parents were opening up in consults. Teens were signing up—and showing up. Lives were being changed and saved *daily.* Prospective coaches were reaching out from across the country, wanting to be part of what we were building.

And I, after everything, was finally ready.
Ready to lead.
Ready to rise.
Ready to believe that maybe the breakdown...wasn't the end.

Maybe it was the beginning all along.

2020 and 2021 weren't just a comeback. **They were magic.**

To this day, Dan, my team, and I still look back on those early years in awe—when Positive Presence transformed from something that belonged to me into something that belonged to *all of us.*

It was no longer just a company. It was a collective heartbeat. A shared light. A movement that reminded me that even when everything feels shattered, you're still allowed to believe.

A Photo I Posted in 2021 Sharing Gratitude for Our Team

Not because you know it'll work. But because something inside you refuses to stay buried.

Because sometimes, belief isn't logical.

It's cellular.

An instinct.

A flicker.

A *knowing*.

And that kind of belief - a stubborn hope that despite insurmountable odds, will never die - is called **sisu**.

The Strength of Stubborn Hope

There's a word in Finnish—*sisu*. It doesn't translate easily, because it isn't just a word. It's a force. Sisu is the quiet, relentless strength that shows up when all signs say give up—and you don't.

It is soul-deep grit. You continue, not because you're certain it will work, but because you know who you are, and quitting isn't it.

I didn't know the term back then, when I felt the walls crashing in around me. But I've felt sisu in my bones my whole life, a stubborn character trait passed down from my father, who no doubt must have had the most *sisu*.

Sisu isn't glamorous. It's not polished or poetic. It's not the victory post or the standing ovation.

It's crying behind the wheel, and still showing up for the meeting. It's walking into a room with puffy eyes and trembling hands, but your head still held high. It's calling Dan with the last credit card you hadn't maxed out. It's whispering, *"I still believe in this,"* even when your voice is hoarse from holding back tears.

It reminds me of the parable of the stonecutter. A man strikes the rock 100 times with no visible change. But on the 101st blow, the stone splits clean in two, not because of that one strike, but because of all the ones that came before it.

The ones no one applauded. The ones no one saw. The ones that looked like they didn't matter—but actually meant everything.

And this is where *sisu* meets your **Witness**. Because somewhere, deep inside—behind the fear, behind the fatigue—is that part of you who is always watching. The presence who sees without judgment. Who whispers, *"Keep going. I see you. And I've got you."*

When the world forgets your name...your Witness remembers your worth. When your hope is flickering...your Witness holds the flame. And when you want to walk away...it gently places your hand back on the hammer.

That's how we keep building. That's how the dream survives. Not through perfection, but through presence. Through one more swing. One more call. One more day of believing.

Even when the dream feels too heavy to carry, Witness reminds us: *You are not alone in this.*

You were never just the stonecutter. You were the stone, the swing, and the steady hand that refused to give up.

I know this because I've lived it.

As my own dream began to root again, I realized: I wasn't just rebuilding a business—I was becoming someone new.

And like anything that's outgrown its container, it was time for me to find a bigger pot.

The Plant and the Pot

Around the time Positive Presence began flourishing again, I was reminded of a plant I had adored when Adam and I were first married in Colorado.

Me and My Cherished 1st Plant

I never gave her a name, but she was definitely a *she*.

I tended to her obsessively—watering her, dusting her leaves, even talking to her.

This was very strange for me because I never had a green thumb, but there was something about this plant that gave me purpose in that moment.

She started small, but then began to flourish...which seemed like magic, considering I had never been able to keep a plant alive before.

One day, her beautiful leaves began to brown. She wilted. And no matter how I cared for her, she withered. Desperate to save her, I took her to a greenhouse.

The horticulturist looked at her and said, "There's nothing wrong with your care. The roots are suffocating. It's outgrown its pot."

And then, right in front of me, the horticulturist began tearing at her roots. "Wait—won't that hurt her?" I asked.

She smiled gently and said something so story-book perfect, it has stayed with me for years: "Sometimes, to grow, you have to leave parts behind."

That lesson hit me like a spiritual freight train.

I use this analogy with my students when they begin to think about what their lives will look like in the future as they continue to grow.

We all have moments where we're being called into a bigger pot—into a new phase, a wider capacity, a version of life that demands more space. And yet we resist. We cling to our current form, even as it suffocates us.

But true growth isn't comfortable.
It's disruptive.
It's messy.
It's heartbreaking.

It means letting go of parts of ourselves that we thought we needed...to become who we are *actually* meant to be.

Sometimes you have to tear the roots. Sometimes you have to leave behind the old pot. Even when it's beautiful. Even when it's all you've ever known.

Fear has a way of convincing us that growth means abandonment. That if we let go of the people, roles, or patterns that shaped us, we'll lose ourselves too. It whispers that without those roots—those titles, those relationships, those identities—we'll be lost. Alone. Unlovable.

But the truth is, you're not letting go of who you are. You're releasing the version of you that once fit—the container that carried you this far, but can no longer hold the fullness of who you're becoming.

We cling because it's familiar.
We cling because it once kept us safe.
We cling because change, even when it's right, can feel like grief.

But growth asks us to trust the unknown. To believe that our roots will take hold again—even in unfamiliar soil.

That tension you feel? It's not failure.

It's the edge of who you've been...meeting who you're becoming. And sometimes, the bravest thing you can do is loosen your grip—Not because you're giving up, but because you're ready to make space for what's next.

A Commitment to Self

In 2023, I replanted into my next pot.

I decided to pursue a yearlong leadership program through the National Women's Impact Leadership Institute (NWILI). It was equal parts brutal and brilliant.

We didn't talk about business. We talked about *self*. We peeled back the layers—how we lead, how we love, how we hide.

Every Thursday for a year, I committed to being a student. I showed up ready to work, bright-eyed and fully open to exploring whatever needed to come.

I strived to be the best student I possibly could. It was mentally exhausting and emotionally raw, but I committed fully to my nine-person cohort and, most importantly, to myself.

Because deep down, I knew: to keep growing, I had to re-pot.

Positive Presence had grown rapidly during the pandemic—almost too rapidly to process. We were in full expansion mode: hiring new coaches, refining our certification program, and scaling operations. From the outside, it looked like we were thriving. And in many ways, we were.

As the sole owner and decision-maker, *I* was struggling to catch my breath. While the company was gaining momentum, I felt like I was sprinting just to keep up. The growth was exciting, but also destabilizing. It swept us forward, fast. But somewhere in that momentum, I lost my footing.

My First Day of NWILI - 2023

I realized that if I wanted to sustain the company's growth—if I wanted to *lead* through it, not just *survive* it—I had to do more than build a bigger business. I had to become a stronger version of myself.

As a founder.

As a female leader.

As a coach.

As a woman.

The next leap wasn't just about growing Positive Presence. It was about growing *me*.

That's when I felt called to take the biggest leap yet: opening Positive Presence's national headquarters. A brick-and-mortar space. A physical home for a vision that had outgrown the confines of my comfort zone. But that decision required something I hadn't accessed in a long time: *courage grounded in clarity.*

So I went inward.

Through my year with NWILI, I did the deep, uncomfortable work of self-excavation. And from that season, something powerful emerged:

My Grand Vision Manifesto—a ten-year map of who I wanted to become, what I wanted to build, and a strategic outline to get Positive Presence to that grand vision of eradicating teenage suicide globally by 2035.

I reverse-engineered everything I wanted for myself—including writing this book—into micro-actions I could take every day. It was a profound discovery to uncover the pot I'm growing into.

And suddenly, I had something I hadn't had in what felt like years: *unshakable direction with defined stepping stones.*

It gave me the courage to move forward, even when the path was messy or unclear. I wasn't waiting for life to calm down or for conditions to be perfect. I was learning to move forward through the uncertainty, trusting myself to handle what came.

Because when you finally know where you're headed, you stop fearing the challenges, and you start meeting them with strength. There's this beautiful metaphor I love about buffalo.

When a storm is coming, most animals run away from it. They try to outpace it, to escape the chaos.

But buffalo?

They run straight into it. They know the fastest way through the storm... is through it.

That's how I see life now, and all the challenges it throws my way. Not as something to avoid, but something to embrace. Not as a path of ease, but a path of evolution.

I've walked into every storm that has ever tried to stop me—debt, rejection, burnout, self-doubt—and I've emerged stronger every single time.

Not because I had a plan. But because I had presence. Because I refused to sit in the pain and call it permanent.

When you stop resisting the storm and start moving with it, something powerful happens.

You discover that the storm isn't there to destroy you—it's there to refine you, like a river smoothing a rock into a stone. Resistance is fear in disguise. But presence?

Presence is magic.

And when you choose presence over panic, you don't just survive the storm—you rise through it. You become the calm within it. You alchemize it.

And from there, everything begins to change.

It's Time to Rise

Even after all the growth, all the healing, all the success—here's the rawest truth of this chapter:

I still sometimes forget to choose myself.

I pour into my students, my team, my family.
I build.
I lead.
I mother.
I love.

And yet, there are days I wake up and realize: I've left me behind. I've become so entangled in my purpose, so wrapped in the roles and titles I carry, that I'm not always sure who I am without them.

So now, I'm learning—slowly, tenderly—to choose myself, too.

To sit with the question, "Who is Michelle Marie King?" Not the CEO. Not the wife. Not the mother. Just the soul. The girl. The woman in the mirror.

I don't know her fully yet. But I'm meeting her in every word of this book. In every root I pull up. In every storm I step into. In every truth I dare to say out loud.

And maybe you're here too.

Maybe you're standing at the edge of something you can't name. Maybe you've outgrown your pot. Maybe you're eyeing the storm. Maybe you're bone-tired and the only thing you have left is one more try.

So try. Choose one next brave thing.
Make the call.
Believe in yourself.
Say yes.
Write the book.
Start the business.
Be brave, get up, put one foot in front of the other, and move forward.

Because you are not your failure. You are not your fear. You are not your most recent mistake. You are the one who decided not to quit.

Let this be your turning point. Let this be the magical moment you choose to rise—not because it's easy, but because it's time.

Reflection Invitations

- What storm are you standing in front of right now? What would it look like to walk through it, not away from it?

- Have you outgrown something in your life? A role, a relationship, a belief? What might it mean to repot?

- What would your Grand Vision Manifesto say if you wrote it today?

- Who are you when you're not producing, performing, or achieving? What parts of you are quietly waiting to be remembered?

6

Rooted In Worth

The moment you begin to heal, a question inevitably arises:
Now what?

After all the unraveling, the releasing, the remembering—what do you do with the you that remains?

The answer, if you listen closely, is simple:

You root. You rise. You build. But this time, you build differently.

This time, you no longer construct your life from a place of scarcity or desperation. You no longer surround yourself with people who only love the broken version of you. You no longer chase fulfillment outside yourself like a mirage, always just out of reach.

You begin, at last, to plant your life in worth—and to build a world around you that reflects who you have always been becoming.

In this beautiful new world, you begin to build, it's important to understand that you also have to make choices, and some of them are really challenging but essential for this new you.

Letting Go of the Tether

Sometimes the first thing we have to do in this new rebuild is to let go. Let go of past beliefs that no longer match the future you're building. Let go of bad habits that once held you back.

And one of the hardest things to let go of, relationships that no longer align with who we are becoming.

I often share this analogy with my students:

Imagine you're climbing a mountain. It's steep, it's wild, and it's yours to climb. But every step forward is met with this tug—a silent, pulling weight tied to your back.

You think it's your backpack. You think it's your own limitation. But then you realize...it's not your gear. It's someone else's tether.

That's how it feels when we cling to relationships that no longer align with our evolution—friendships, partnerships, environments, even identities that once felt safe but are now quietly keeping us stuck.

There have been many seasons in my life where I had to face the truth: someone I cared for deeply was no longer climbing alongside me. And in those moments, I had to make a choice—let them pull me back down the mountain, or cut the tether.

Sometimes, the most radical act of self-respect is letting go. Not in anger. Not in ego. But in honor. Because here's the hard-to-admit truth:

When you finally cut the tether, you don't just feel lighter, you feel stronger. There's a surge of freedom. A flicker of light. And suddenly, the mountain no longer looms as high.

But that decision—to love yourself enough to let go—is an ache filled with meaning. And it is necessary.

The Sisyphus Season

I spent years trying to prove my worth—not just to others, but to myself. Especially after I became an entrepreneur. Especially when the blueprint of worth I had growing up was rooted in someone else's silence.

My relationship with my father was always complicated. As a Navy man, he was disciplined, hard-working, and emotionally distant.

His love didn't show up in words or affection. It showed up in silence. In expectations. In disappointment that never quite made it into language. As a child, I internalized that silence. I mistook it for shame.

I assumed it meant I wasn't enough.

So as I entered the business world, I did what so many of us do with unhealed wounds—I looked for people to heal them for me. I sought out mentors, business partners, authority figures—especially men—hoping they could give me what I never got: Pride. Praise. Belonging.

And for a while, I thought I had found it. Some male role models genuinely saw me. They believed in my ideas. They lifted me with guidance and wisdom.

But there were others—ones who saw the little girl in me still reaching for her father's approval, and they used that hunger as leverage.

They dangled opportunities and withheld praise. They offered conditional affirmation. They played what I now recognize as emotional power games—where I had to constantly prove my value, stay small, or stay grateful just to remain included.

One mentor praised my drive, only to later say I was "too much." Another offered partnership, then cut me out of decisions once the spotlight was his.

Each time, I gave all of me hoping they'd reciprocate. I lost myself over and over again. And when those relationships crumbled—as they inevitably did—I felt like I crumbled with them.

It left me feeling like Sisyphus—the mythical figure doomed to push a boulder up a hill only to watch it roll back down again.

Every time a connection unraveled, every time a promise was broken, my self-worth tumbled with it. Because I had attached it to them. And when they left, they took parts of me with them.

It took years—and a lot of unlearning—to realize that my worth was never theirs to give. That I didn't need another mentor to mirror back my value. I needed to become the mirror.

Eventually, I stopped pushing the boulder. And instead, I transmuted it into a pebble I now carry in my pocket. Not as a weight, but as a reminder:

Of how strong I am.
Of how far I've come.
Of the power I hold when I stop chasing someone else's version of worth...and start reclaiming my own.

Becoming Rooted

Between 2017 and 2019, I entered a season of profound spiritual healing.

By then, I had spent years carrying invisible weight—chasing success, validation, and my worth through the eyes of others. I knew something had to shift, but I didn't yet know how.

Part of that healing came through my work with ayahuasca—an ancient Amazonian plant medicine that's been used in ceremonial rituals for thousands of years.

Traditionally brewed into a thick tea by Indigenous shamans, ayahuasca is made from two sacred plants and is known for its psychoactive properties. But to call it just a "hallucinogen" would be to miss the point entirely.

Ayahuasca isn't about escaping reality—it's about confronting it. Deeply. Directly. Spiritually.

It's often referred to as "Grandmother" or "Abuela" because of the distinctly feminine, wise, and sometimes fierce energy it carries. She is a teacher. A mirror. A guide. Not the gentle, comforting kind—though she can be—but the kind who sits you down, looks you in the eye, and says, "It's time to see what you've been avoiding."

I didn't find ayahuasca casually—I was called to it.

I had been in search of something deeper, something more than talk therapy or meditation or journaling could reach.

Through a series of synchronicities, I found a sacred healing circle led by a trusted shaman named Sam. The ceremony took place in a safe, intentionally held space with a small group of seekers—each of us carrying our own pain, our own questions, our own longing to heal.

And let me tell you—I met my healing with a scream.

In one ceremony, I remember yelling in my mind's eye, in my spirit—**"I am worthy! Can't you see that?!"**

And yet... I didn't see it in myself.

Even in the spirit realm, I was still trying to prove my worth. Still wrestling. Still fighting. But slowly, the lessons softened me.

Ayahuasca didn't hand me my healing in a neat little package. She peeled it back layer by layer—until I could meet myself, not as someone broken or unworthy, but as someone who had always been whole. Just buried beneath the noise.

I learned that the most magnetic people aren't the ones who chase validation—they're the ones who radiate alignment.

And with the help of my shaman, Sam—who held space for the unraveling and reassembling of my soul—I finally understood something that cracked through every layer of my conditioning:

You don't have to prove it. You just have to be it.

Those words didn't just land in my mind. They surged through my bloodstream. They echoed through every memory where I had bent, begged, and broken myself trying to earn the love, respect, and belonging I always deserved simply by existing.

And for the first time in my life, I *believed* them.

I didn't have to overperform. I didn't have to outshine, out-hustle, or out-achieve anyone. I didn't have to twist myself into palatable pieces just to be seen.

I already was.

From that point forward, I stopped chasing the spotlight and started *becoming* the light. I stopped begging the world to notice me and started noticing *myself*. The way I moved. The way I led. The way I loved.

And as I did, something extraordinary happened.

My life began to rearrange itself around this new vibration.

I started attracting people who didn't prey on my insecurities—they honored my sovereignty. Mentors who *poured* into me, not because they wanted control, but because they saw my potential. Partners who weren't threatened by my shine but inspired by it. Clients who came not for perfection, but for presence.

Suddenly, I wasn't surrounded by mirrors of my past pain. I was surrounded by reflections of my current peace. Validation that when you stop auditioning for your worth, the right people stop asking for proof. That's when I knew:

This wasn't just a breakthrough. It was a rebirth.

A Rebirth into Fulfillment

After years of striving—after chasing worth through achievement, validation, and endless forward motion—something inside me finally broke open. Not into pieces. Into possibility.

I had spent so long trying to "arrive" somewhere. To build the perfect life. To become the perfect version of me. But all along, I had mistaken fulfillment for a finish line. A goalpost. A mountaintop moment that would finally make me whole.

What I didn't realize then was that fulfillment doesn't come after you prove yourself. It comes after you *acknowledge* yourself.

After you've let go of the identities you once clung to.
After you've surrendered the striving.
After you've walked through the fire of unlearning.

Then, in the quiet that follows, you begin to fill up. Not from something you find out there, but what you reconnect with in here.

Because fulfillment isn't something the world hands you. It's something that's been **living inside you** all along—waiting for you to stop running long enough to feel it.

By this point in my journey, I had climbed through fear. I had grieved the versions of me that I once believed I had to be. I had shed identities that no longer served me. I had whispered truths I once feared to say out loud.

And now—here—I stood in the space I had created by letting go.
Not searching. Not striving.
Just breathing. Just becoming.

I acknowledged how far I had come. Not in miles or milestones—but in presence. In grace. In wholeness. Because that's what true fulfillment feels like.

It's not the fanfare or applause. It's not the next title or the next launch. It's not perfection.

It's peace.

It's laughter at the dinner table. It's walking barefoot in the backyard. It's the first sip of coffee in a sunlit room. It's the realization that your life no longer needs to look impressive to be meaningful. It just needs to feel true.

And from that place, where nothing was missing and everything belonged, I felt something rise. Not my ego. Not my goals. But my light.

A quiet inner radiance that wasn't fueled by effort, but by alignment. Not by what I was doing, but by how I was being. Not from being seen, but from finally seeing myself clearly.

I was no longer building from fear. I was creating from reverence. And from that place—from the ashes of all I thought I needed to become—I magically emerged.

Not perfect. Not complete. But whole. And I didn't just rise. **I radiated.**

Reflection Invitation

Let the questions that arise throughout this book and this chapter act as a doorway, not a demand. There are no wrong answers. There is only the sacred act of choosing yourself again and again and again.

And then, in that silence—in that fertile, soul-fed stillness—breathe deep. Feel the light returning to your bones. And remember: You are already the home. You are already the answer. You are already the worth you've been waiting for.

- Where in my life have I been chasing external fulfillment instead of nurturing internal peace?

- Who are the five people I am most influenced by right now? Are they aligned with my future or tethered to my past?

- What daily habits, media, and conversations feed my light? What drains it?

- Where am I still waiting for permission to feel worthy? What would change if I decided today that I already am?

- How can I build a life—starting today—that feels like rich, vibrant soil for the dreams I have not yet dared to speak aloud?

7

Positive Presence

We never forget the people who sat with us in our darkest moments—not to fix us, but to witness us. To hold us. To stay. That kind of presence leaves a permanent mark on the soul.

In 2015, I never set out to become a mental health coach for teens. I didn't even know what a 'coach' truly was. I had no personal blueprint—no mentor, no guide, no one who had shown me what it meant to truly help others.

What I did have was pain. A deep, pulsing ache that lived in every corner of my mind. A whisper that was growing louder, saying: there has to be more than this.

More than surface-level conversations. More than a world that asks young people to be perfect while giving them no tools for resilience. More than a life spent hiding in the shadows of who you're supposed to be, instead of discovering who you *actually* are.

And what I lacked in experience, I made up for in empathy.

My model coaching program in those early days began with a structured, topic-based curriculum. I found myself listening more than teaching. Conversations turned into coaching. Lessons turned into life experiences. They opened their hearts, and I recognized pieces of my younger self in every word.

That was the moment something inside me shifted. They didn't need another instructor. They needed a mentor. And maybe—just maybe—I could be that.

I remember the exact moment the realization hit. That what I was doing with these girls was about so much more than teaching modeling technique.

I was standing in my living room in Castle Rock, CO, the reality of this new chapter as a business owner still weighing heavily on my heart (and my bank account).

My mind wandered back to a conversation I'd had with a student the day before—how she had opened up about always feeling unsure of herself. I remember feeling proud, knowing I had offered her something real, tangible guidance, a place to land, a way forward.

And then, almost without warning, it dawned on me:

I had crossed a threshold.

This was no longer just about modeling technique. It was about connection, transformation, belonging. And from that moment on, I knew there was no going back. So I walked away. From the modeling industry. From pageants, from my role as a modeling coach. Because I wasn't just teaching models anymore.

I was holding lives in my hands.

This was a new kind of relationship—the birth of what I would one day call: **mentor-coaching.** A sacred space where we don't just talk at students—we *collaborate* with them. Where we don't just listen—we *connect*. Where we don't just coach—we *guide* our students through some of the most challenging moments of their lives.

In those early years, I was fumbling my way forward right beside them. Every time I taught a student something about worth or purpose, I was whispering it back into the wounded places in myself. It was a sacred partnership of becoming, both theirs and mine.

The Butterfly Effect

Mentor-coaching isn't about fixing people. It's not about shouting affirmations until they stick or dishing advice from a mountaintop of success. It's the quiet art of standing beside someone as they crawl into their cocoon—raw, undone, full of questions—and patiently waiting with them as they crystallize.

I often share the butterfly metaphor with my students. When a caterpillar enters the chrysalis, it doesn't just sprout wings. It *dissolves*, breaking down into a shapeless soup of cells before becoming something entirely new.

And within that chaos live *imaginal discs*—the blueprint of the butterfly, quietly waiting, present all along, even when the caterpillar had no idea what it was becoming.

That's what mentor-coaching is. We don't rush transformation. We sit beside it. We hold space for the blueprint when our students only feel the goo. We remind them gently, as many times as we need to:

You are not broken. You are becoming.

I always tell them: "You are the caterpillar. The cocoon. The gooey, uncertain middle. One day, you'll emerge as the butterfly. And when you do, the world will shift in your wake."

But here's what I didn't understand back then: Sometimes, when you step into the role of the cocoon—when you hold someone through their most fragile becoming—you discover that the work isn't just about transformation.

Sometimes, it's about survival.

The Moment I Became a Lifeline

It was a perfect Colorado summer day in 2017 at one of my student's homes. We were mid-session at one of our partner-led art therapy workshops. The topic was teen stress—bullying, anxiety, insecurity—and we were using creativity to help students express what they couldn't always say aloud.

Then, we reached the subject of teen suicide. I asked gently, "Have you ever felt like hurting yourself?"

Expecting an immediate 'no' from this particular student who was a beautiful, bubbly, bright, hilarious, emotionally mature 11-year old girl. She paused. Nodded.

"Yes."

Time stopped.

She described—so quietly, so clearly—the day she came home from school after being bullied, grabbed a kitchen knife, and sat in her closet. How she imagined where she'd cut. She thought about how the knife might feel against her skin. How she didn't go through with it...but how the idea had never really left.

Under the table, I squeezed the hand of my friend, the art therapist who came to that session with me to do a personal development project after my section of the session. I squeezed so tightly trying to channel all of my emotion into my grip—I left marks.

I listened. I validated. I asked the really hard questions that someone needed to ask to ensure she was in a safe place with herself. I kept my voice calm, my emotional response neutral.

And after connecting my student with the support she needed, and having a long conversation with her parents, I got into my car, drove down the road, pulled over, and screamed until I couldn't breathe.

That day broke me. And it built me. That was the day Positive Presence stopped being a business. It became a **lifeline.**

It was the moment I realized: This work doesn't just matter. It saves lives.

The True Meaning

Mentor-coaching isn't a job. It's a calling. A way of *being.*

It's sharing your story so someone else doesn't feel alone in theirs. It's holding space for a fear without needing to fix it. It's giving someone stability when they need it, and honest reflection when they're ready for it. It's celebrating the "aha" moments—and honoring every breakdown on the way there.

Most of our students live in the *messy middle*—between who they've been told to be and who they long to become. What they need isn't another adult handing down advice or giving orders. What they need is someone to say: *Let's figure this out. Together.*

True mentorship goes beyond advice—it lays the foundation for transformation. It's about *witnessing.* We hold students the way you'd hold a butterfly—delicately, reverently, knowing you may never fully see the impact, but trusting it was sacred all the same.

And then there are the students who leave more than an imprint. They leave a legacy.

For me, that student was Marek. And he changed everything for me.

The Lost Life

Marek Edwin Putman
08/13/2001-05/13/2018

Marek was one of my very first students, back when I was still focused on model coaching.

He wasn't just radiant; he was a force. His smile could stop traffic. His hugs wrapped around your entire soul. His presence lit up any room he entered. He was mischief and magic, all in one.

And on Mother's Day 2018, the world lost him to suicide.

What followed wasn't just grief. It was fury. It was helplessness. It was heartbreak with no place to go.

I remember the moment I found out.

It was as if the air changed, the room shifted, and suddenly, the world no longer fit around me. And in the silence of this new reality without Marek, a vow rose in me like wildfire.

There was no hiding anymore. No shrinking back. No waiting for someone else to step up.

I sat on the floor, surrounded by the pieces of the business I thought I had built—and for the first time, I looked past the surface and saw what it was truly meant to become.

This wasn't just a program. It was a *promise.*

A promise to see the ones slipping quietly into the shadows. To hear the ones who had stopped speaking—not just to others, but to themselves. To fight for them until they could remember how to fight for themselves.

That was the day everything shifted. That was the day I stopped being a coach with a business— and became a mentor-coach with a mission.

Not by choice. By necessity. By sacred assignment. From that day forward, I knew this work could no longer be reactive.

It had to be *revolutionary.*

Because Marek wasn't an outlier—he was a reflection of a system that's failing too many. If we want to prevent more stories like his, we have to look beyond coaching...we have to reshape the future entirely.

Weaving Compassion

The truth is, our education system doesn't teach self-discovery.

We reward performance over presence. We celebrate test scores, not emotional safety. We teach formulas and facts—but not how to sit with grief. Not how to navigate shame. Not how to love ourselves.

In a world where one in three high school students report persistent feelings of sadness or hopelessness, and suicide remains the leading cause of death for youth ages 10–24 in the U.S., we have to ask:

What are we *really* teaching our kids to value?

The system is built to sort, not to support. To push outcomes, not inner clarity. Students are praised for their productivity, but rarely asked how they're doing underneath the surface. And as a result, too many of them are drowning silently behind straight A's and smiling selfies.

One of my former students had a perfect transcript—and a collapsing inner world. Straight A's. Leadership roles. Scholarship offers. And yet, beneath it all, he was cracking under the pressure to be perfect. No one had ever taught him he was worthy without the accolades.

In our sessions, he cried for the first time in years. He softened. He let himself be seen. And for the first time, with someone who saw *him*—not just his résumé—he began to believe he was enough.

With that unconditional support, he started building a life that felt right on the inside, not just impressive on paper.

This is what mentor-coaching creates: A space for students to stop performing and start becoming. We give them permission to be real, to question what success truly means to them and to define themselves by more than a resume or a GPA.

My vision?

It's not about fighting the system. It's about weaving something more compassionate through it—a new thread of humanity, presence, and purpose.

A future where emotional intelligence is valued as highly as academic achievement. Where every school integrates life literacy—equipping teens to process emotions, communicate with empathy, set boundaries, pursue purpose, and regulate their nervous system.

Where mentorship is embedded into every student's experience, not as an intervention, but as a foundation. Where "success" is redefined to include fulfillment, mental health, and self-worth, not just college acceptances and stacked resumes.

Where students don't just graduate with a diploma—they graduate with a deeper understanding of who they are.

This isn't idealistic. It's necessary. And it starts with one safe space. One trusted adult. One student who finally feels seen.

Because when we prioritize presence over performance, we don't just raise test scores—we raise a generation that knows how to love, lead, and live from a place of wholeness.

And, at the end of the day, isn't that the whole point?

The Light in the Dark

There's a myth we've been sold: That we have to be fully healed before we're allowed to help others. That we must wait until we have all the answers to show up for someone else. But I've learned this isn't true.

Some of the most transformative moments I've had as a coach didn't happen when I felt strong—they happened when I was still learning how to love myself. When I was unraveling. When I had no plan, only presence.

Because real resilience isn't fearlessness. It's choosing to carry the light...even while walking through the dark.

At first, that light—*my why*—was my daughter. I wanted to change the generation she would one day look up to. To offer her a world filled with kind, conscious, emotionally aware role models.

Savannah & I - 2021

But then I met *them*. The teens and young adults who walk through our doors each day. The ones who reminded me of a younger version of myself—before I had the words, the tools, the truth.

And that's when I realized: I couldn't just build a better world for her. I had to build it for *them*, too. For today's youth, what we call the **Next Generation.**

A generation between 12 and 24 years old who are deeply in-tuitive, incredibly empathetic, and beautifully self-aware. And yet, so many of them are silently drowning in shame, pressure, perfectionism, and self-doubt. They are praised for their per-formance, but rarely seen for who they really are.

So I created Positive Presence not just to help them cope, but to help them transform.

We do that by training mentor-coaches to walk beside them, not in front of them. By creating spaces where emotional intel-ligence is foundational. By teaching the tools a lot of us adults never had growing up—self-awareness, executive functioning, positive psychology, and unconditional belonging.

But here's the bigger vision—our *loftiest* goal. One we speak about often inside Positive Presence, but rarely outside of it:

We're not just coaching this generation. We're raising the ones who will raise the next. This is our swan song. The dream be-neath the dream.

One day, the students we coach today (those 12-24 year olds) will grow up and become the parents of the **Positive Presence Generation.**

The Positive Presence Generation will be born into homes where emotional intelligence is modeled daily. Where worth is not earned—it's remembered. Where parents become mentors. Where trauma is not passed down, but processed and healed.

Imagine a world where our children no longer need coaching to *remember* who they are...because they were never asked to forget. Where self-love and self-respect are inherited. Where executive functioning and emotional regulation are dinner table conversations. Where compassion isn't taught through crisis, it's woven into the rhythm of family life.

That is the Positive Presence Generation.

And the work we do today—every session, every connection, every life we touch—is preparing the soil for that future. Because if we can help this generation become cycle-breakers, they will raise a generation that doesn't need to repair brokenness.

They will raise a generation that begins in the light. A generation born into a world and a family of self-love, emotional fluency, and pure potentiality.

This is our long game. My team and I are planting seeds we may never see fully bloom. And still, we plant them. Because one day, this work will no longer be necessary.

And that will be the greatest sign of its success.

The Positive Presence Generation is coming. And when they arrive, we'll know...we didn't just light the path, we helped build the world they'll rise in.

And it will be nothing short of revolutionary.

Our Stars – A Poem for My Students

There have been moments in this work when the weight feels unbearable. When the world outside is loud and heavy...and my inner fire flickers low.

But then—I remember them. The quiet breakthroughs. The brave confessions. The soft smiles that speak louder than words.

I remember the ones who showed up even when they didn't want to. The ones who cried in silence before they ever spoke aloud. The ones who reminded me—that this work isn't about fixing, it's about witnessing.

I wrote this poem for them. For every student who trusted me with their light, even when they didn't yet believe it was there. They are my stars—constant, luminous, and wildly unique. And every time I feel lost in the dark...I look up and remember exactly why I do what I do. This piece is called: **"Our Stars."**

It's my love letter to the light we build together—and the future they'll carry forward.

When the world is against me
And there's not much light to see
I look around at all the stars
Finding their place in the sky around me

These pieces of light
Of Hope and Peace

A wave of impact
I can't wait to see

They ebb and flow
With my contrasting sky
When I'm in light, I shine for them
And in my dark, they become my why

He's the life I saved
She's the girl I made smile
He's the challenging one that let me in
She's the one that found her purpose...
...and it's okay that it took a while

Just like them I am a student
Of everything they share
For a mentor can only become great
When their mentee becomes aware

Aware of the world AROUND them
And how little is in their control
Aware of the world WITHIN them
And how much power they truly hold

From sparks to a flame
To a ball of light
They begin to radiate with purpose and passion
And begin to shine bright

Until their power could no longer be contained within
That new found joy for life
Expands to the world outside of them

A beaming light
A ripple effect
One strong voice
And one small step

So here I stand amazed of that light
One proud, awe-inspired mentor
Wishing that it will always shine bright

Reflection Invitations

- Who has mentored you—formally or quietly behind the scenes? What did they awaken in you?

- If you could become the mentor you always needed, what would that look like?

- Where in your life are you being invited to be present, rather than perfect?

- Have you had a "Marek Moment"—a wake-up call that redefined your why?

- If you could whisper one message to the next generation, what would it be?

- What part of your metamorphosis are you in? What's one belief or identity you're ready to shed as you grow wings?

8

A Legacy of Light

There's a question I ask myself often—not just in the quiet of my soul, but in the fabric of how I live, lead, and love:

What will remain when I'm gone?

Not the titles. Not the trophies. Not the carefully curated online footprint. But the real legacy—the invisible imprint. The echo of presence that lingers long after I'm no longer here.

That, to me, is what legacy truly is. Not what we leave behind, but what we leave *within* the lives we've touched. And I believe the most powerful legacies aren't built through perfection, but through presence.

Spreading Positivity

Years ago, when I first launched Positive Presence, I scribbled a line in my notebook that still moves through every breath of my work:

"Positivity can only spread when it is present."

At the time, I thought it was just a tagline—a pretty sentence to sum up a feeling. But now, I see it as something much bigger. A truth. A calling. A reminder.

Because positivity—real, anchored, embodied positivity—is not just about smiling or staying upbeat. It's about being fully *here*. With yourself. With others. With the moment.

And when you live from that kind of anchored presence, your energy becomes contagious. Not in a performative, loud way. But in a *magnetic*, soul-deep, cellular way.

You become the lighthouse. And remind others they are light, too. That's the heartbeat behind the **Plus Sign Movement**—an idea I dreamed into being years ago, born from a vision to make positivity visible. Tangible. Shareable.

It started with something simple: With two fingers in the form of a plus sign. Then it quickly went viral with people from all over the world sending in pictures of hidden plus signs drawn on their hand, sketched on a napkin or chalked on a sidewalk.

My Launch of the Plus Sign Movement - 2017

These quiet symbols of support in 2017 were kind messages of presence, of *"I see you"*, in a world that so often doesn't. I still believe that movement can go viral again—not just on social media, but in spirit. Not just in hashtags, but in hearts.

Because what if every person carried a plus sign in their mind's eye, a small, sturdy reminder that they matter? That they belong? That their presence is exactly what the world needs right now?

The Magic of Belief

There's a study I once read that I've never been able to forget.

In 1957, a Harvard researcher named Dr. Curt Richter placed rats in a tank of water to test how long they could tread before drowning. On average, they lasted about 15 minutes. But just before they gave up—right before surrender—he pulled them out. Dried them off. Let them rest.

Then, he placed them back in the water. The second time, the rats didn't tread for 15 minutes. They treaded for 60 hours.

Sixty hours.

The only thing that changed? They believed rescue was possible. They believed survival was worth it. That is the power of belief. That is the power of presence.

Belief doesn't erase struggle—but it changes what's possible inside it. That is also the power of presence. Because sometimes, belief isn't born from within. Sometimes, it's borrowed from someone who sees your fight. Someone who pulls you from the water just long enough for you to remember that rescue is real.

We are all in our own oceans. And some days, the thing that keeps us afloat isn't strength—it's memory. The memory that we have been saved before. That someone showed up. That someone believed.

I want to be that someone. I want you to be that someone—for yourself, and for the people treading quietly beside you. Because when belief enters the room, impossibility magically has no choice but to leave.

Something Unfamiliar

I once wrote this in a journal during a season of quiet reflection:

> *"Is it weird that I always talk about acclimating to a journey as it gets harder? How is it that my journey in this moment in time feels more seamless and beautiful? There is no struggle. It almost feels like I'm flying over my journey instead of climbing it."*

That day in the winter of 2022, I experienced something unfamiliar: peace. Not the kind of peace I had to earn. Not the kind I had to force, chase, or fake. But a quiet, embodied peace—the kind that hums beneath the noise. The kind that just *is*.

It arrived during one of the most draining seasons I'd lived through in years. Business demands were mounting. I felt stretched thin between expansion and exhaustion.

We were hiring, launching, scaling—all while I was still grieving the loss of my father, still healing, still trying to hold space for others while learning how to hold space for myself.

Everything *should* have felt heavy. And yet—that morning, something in me felt light.

I was alone in the kitchen. The house still quiet. A steaming cup of coffee warmed my palms. My journal lay open, but for once, I wasn't writing to process or plan. I wasn't searching for answers. I was simply... present.

Then, I looked out the window and saw them—six deer crossing the frozen pond behind our house. Now, deer aren't rare where we live. But this sighting felt different.

They weren't in a hurry. They weren't afraid. They moved slowly, gracefully—fully aware of their surroundings, yet completely unbothered by them.

And in that moment, I understood something:

Peace isn't something you force. It's something you allow.

For so long, I had treated peace like a reward—something waiting at the end of achievement. A destination reserved for vacations, sabbaticals, retreats.

Something I could earn after proving myself enough times, fixing enough things, helping enough people. But that day, I didn't do anything extraordinary.

I just *noticed*. I breathed slower. I sipped softer. I let my shoulders drop, my jaw unclench. I allowed myself to be human—not in the process of becoming, but in the quiet beauty of *being*. No performance. No proving. Just presence.

And that, I now know, is what observance of peace really means. It's not about controlling the moment. It's about releasing your grip long enough to realize you're safe inside of it.

Peace isn't always a grand epiphany or perfect stillness. Sometimes it's just the willingness to *witness* your life, to surrender—without running from it.

That winter morning became a turning point for me. Because once I felt that kind of peace—not circumstantial, but cellular—I knew I could return to it anytime I chose. And maybe that's the most powerful thing I've learned:

Peace is not a place. It's a practice. A remembering.

You don't need to climb the whole mountain to earn rest. You can be the eagle—soaring above it—simply because you *allowed* yourself to.

And just like the deer gliding across the ice, unhurried and undisturbed, you can meet your life with grace. Not because it's easy, but because you finally stopped making yourself earn what was always yours to hold.

Curious, I Googled the spiritual meaning of deer. *Peace. Tranquility. Graceful action. Self-awareness. Connection to subtle energies.* Every sign in that moment was pointing to one thing:

Pause is Presence. Presence is Peace.

The deeper I leaned into my spiritual self, the clearer it became—*Positive Presence* is not just a brand. It is not just my business. It's a mirror.

Like all the other mirrors that came before it, it was a living reflection of my own journey. It's the part of me that remembers magic when the world forgets. My twin flame. My soul's work. My offering.

When she grows, I grow. When I breathe, she breathes. When I heal, she heals. The more I become myself, the more she becomes what she was meant to be.

Your Light, Your Truth

As Positive Presence continued to grow in the early 2020s, my leadership team and I spoke often of the metaphorical mountain our students climb with their Positive Presence mentor-coach.

We all vow to help our students climb it, not just with instruction, but with presence. We do not carry them. We walk beside them. Until they, too, proclaim: *I am enough.* And then, the work doesn't leave us when the session ends. The students don't leave us when the program is over.

They remain—energetically. Imprinted. Woven into our hearts. Their growth becomes our growth. Their transformation becomes our testament.

A Living Legacy

I want to leave behind a belief that we are all made of light and magic. That we are here not to *earn* our worth, but to remember it. That when we stop chasing, comparing, shrinking, we begin to glow.

Let it be a world where positivity isn't just a platitude, but a way of life.

Where teenagers say, *"I am enough,"* with their full chests. Where parents lead with presence, not pressure. Where belief isn't rare—it's radiant.

Let it be the Plus Sign drawn on the hand of a teenager who finally feels seen. Let it be the mentor-coach who shows up—rain or shine—because belief matters.

Let it be the light we pass from hand to hand, heart to heart, until the whole world glows.

And let my legacy be this:
That I dared to believe in people.
That I stayed in the room with them.
That I was the presence that helped them remember their own.
Because one day, when I am long gone, I want someone to say:

"She loved hard. She believed fully. She showed up when it mattered. She was—and always will be—a positive presence!"

That, to me, is enough.

Reflection Invitations

- What kind of legacy are you leaving behind—in your family, your work, your energy?

- Where in your life are you being called to show up with presence instead of perfection?

- If positivity can only spread when it is present, where are you being asked to be more present?

- What belief are you willing to hold, even when the world tells you it's impossible?

- Who in your life has been your "plus sign"? And who can you be that for today?

9

Conclusion: The Alchemy

There are some moments in life, quiet, unannounced, when you look around and realize: You made it through. Not to the end. But to a clearing on your path, a perfect place to stop, rest, observe, and appreciate everything you'd accomplished and gone through up to this point.

There, you will find the beginning of knowing yourself. Trusting yourself. Honoring yourself. The beginning of becoming the person you were always meant to be. Not in spite of your pain, but because of it. Not in perfection, but in presence.

This is your alchemy. The magic of turning ache into art. Doubt into devotion. Wounds into wisdom. Of finding the sacred in the mundane, the extraordinary in the everyday, and the light even in the dark.

You've traveled through storms and awakenings, grief and grace, unraveling and becoming. You've faced fear, reclaimed your worth, questioned the systems that shaped you, and remembered the magic that was always within you.

You've walked beside me as I turned pain into purpose and built a life, a legacy, and a movement from the pieces I once thought were too broken to hold.

And now here you are—whole, radiant, and rising. This is the moment where most books end. But you and I both know this isn't an ending. It's a beginning.

A beginning of a life rooted in presence and led by possibility. A life shaped not by who the world told you to be, but by who your soul already knows you are. A life where you don't wait for permission to be powerful. You just are. This is your moment to step into your magic.

To become your own alchemist—a sacred transformer of pain into beauty, fear into fuel, and wounds into wisdom. To look back on all that shaped you, not with shame, but with reverence. Because every heartbreak carved a deeper well for love. Every challenge gave you new strength. Every stumble made you softer. And every part of your story was preparing you to rise into this version of yourself.

You don't have to be perfect to begin. You don't need to have it all figured out. The truth is, you are already everything you seek. The presence. The purpose. The peace. It's all inside you. It always has been.

All that's left now... is to believe it. To live it. To spread the magic that lives inside you. Because positivity can only spread when it is present. So radiate it. Let it ripple. Let it become your legacy.

Wisdom to Live By

Throughout this book, you've walked beside me through storms and stillness, heartbreak and hope. You've witnessed the messy miracle of transformation—and perhaps felt your own. As we near the close of this shared journey, I want to offer you ten truths that have shaped my life, guided my healing, and anchored my soul.

These are not rules. They are reminders. Echoes of lessons I've lived, whispered back to you as gentle invitations to remember who you are and what you're made of. Let them be your compass—steady, unwavering—when the world tries to pull you off course.

"I stopped looking for the light and decided to become the light instead." Fulfillment doesn't come from chasing something external—it's born from the moment you realize the radiance has always been within. You are the source, not the seeker.

"Positivity can only spread when it is present." If you want to change the world, start by tending to your own energy. Light spreads not through force, but through presence.

"What if being lost is the path that leads to being found?" We often fear disorientation, but the truth is: the map of your soul is drawn in the darkness. Trust the wandering. It's how you build the strength to love yourself through the becoming, and realize that *you* are the home you've been searching for all along.

"The sun never wonders why it was cloudy yesterday, it's just focused on shining today!" Let go of the weight of what was. Shine today. Shine despite the rain. Again and again.

"The more you root yourself in your truth, the harder it becomes to be shaken." Resilience grows when you honor your choices and stand behind them. Confidence isn't about having all the answers; it's about staying present, grounded, and aligning with who you are.

"Care but don't carry." Loving someone deeply doesn't mean losing yourself in their struggle. You can hold space for others without holding their pain as your own.

"Perfection isn't about being perfect all the time, it's about accepting who you are today." Your worth has never depended on your performance. It's found in the radical act of self-acceptance.

"You're never going to know how strong you are until you're given an opportunity to see how strong you are." Life doesn't test you to break you. It tests you to reveal you. Let hardship unveil the warrior within.

"A lot of people find their passion, not so many find their purpose, and very few people leave a legacy." Passion ignites. Purpose directs. But legacy? That's the light you leave behind in others. Make your life about finding that purpose and it absolutely WILL become the life you're looking for!

"Gratitude is the bridge to love." When you learn to be grateful for even the smallest breath, you begin to open yourself to everything sacred. Gratitude expands your capacity to love—and to be love. These truths are yours now. Hold them close. Share them widely. Let them grow.

The Legacy of Light

I've spoken a lot in these pages about pain. About struggle. About the moments I wanted to give up and the people who helped me find my way back. And there's two relationships I want to honor—openly, honestly, and with a full heart.

I've written about my father with deep vulnerability. I've shared wounds that shaped me, absences that hurt, silence that echoed through my childhood.

But I want to be crystal clear: Being his daughter was one of the greatest honors of my life.

My father was laid to rest at Arlington National Cemetery with full military honors. He served this country for 23 years in the Navy. He was a hero. He was also a human—a man carrying pain he didn't know how to name, doing the best he could with what he had. And even in his hardest moments, he kept me safe. He was my anchor. My reminder that I, too, could be strong.

And my mother! She is the angel on earth who continues to walk beside me through every storm. Her quiet strength, her unwavering love, her resilience in the face of impossibility—that is the fire I carry in my soul.

They are my roots. My wings. My why.

Sometimes we expect our parents to be perfect. To know us. To never falter. But we forget—they are growing, too. They are fighting their own battles while trying to love us the best they know how.

Give them grace. Love them anyways.

The Magic You Carry

You were never meant to walk through life untouched by hardship. You were meant to learn from it. To alchemize it. To turn every scar into gold.

An alchemist is not someone who avoids pain—they are someone who transforms through it. An alchemist turns grief into depth, fear into faith, pain into *purpose*.

They hold the world gently. Love fiercely. And leave behind not just footsteps, but frequencies—echoes of light that guide others home.

You are that. You are the legacy. You are the movement. You are the presence.

So walk boldly into your next chapter, not with fear, but with magic. Not with a script, but with a spark. And know this:

You were never lost. You were always becoming.

Now it's your turn to shine. Let your light be contagious. Let your presence be the revolution. Let your life be the greatest spell you ever cast.

And if you forget? Just return to this truth:

'Positivity can only spread when it is present.'

Be present...and the **MAGIC** will follow.

Acknowledgements

For every soul who walked beside me—thank you for helping me rise.

To **Adam,** My lighthouse in every storm. Thank you for being the one soul I've never had to question. Your quiet strength, steady support, and unwavering love have held me together in every chapter—especially the ones I wasn't sure I could finish. You saw my worth long before I did, and you reminded me that true love is a place to rest, not something to earn. This book exists because you made space for me to write it—not just with time, but with trust.

To **Savannah,** My magic girl. You are the spark that ignited all of this. Becoming your mother was the turning point of my life—my reason to rise, my reminder to return to the light. Every page of this book carries your name, whether it's written or not. I hope one day you read these words and remember: you were born of magic—and that magic lives in you, always.

To **my parents,** Thank you for the love you gave and the lessons you never knew you were teaching. Mom—your resilience and grace have always been my foundation. In every storm, you stood steady. You taught me how to rise with dignity, how to love without limits, and how to keep showing up. Dad—your silence shaped me, but so did your quiet strength. In our final moments together, without words, you gave me everything I needed: your presence. I carry you both in everything I do.

To **my team at Positive Presence,** You are the heartbeat of this movement. Cheyanne, Mira, Lori, Eduardo, Nadine, Dan, Mark, Wendy, all of my amazing peers that preceded you, and the entire past, present & future global coaching team—thank you. Thank you for believing in the impossible right alongside me. For choosing courage when comfort would have been easier. For bringing your brilliance, your grit, and your full hearts to this mission every single day. You don't just work with me; you *walk alongside me.*

To **my students,** Since 2013, I have had the immense honor to work with thousands of tweens, teens and young adults. EVERY SINGLE ONE OF YOU has been my greatest teacher. Thank you for letting me witness your unraveling and your rising. Your stories live inside every chapter of this book—your tears, your courage, your light. This book isn't just about me. It's about us. You reminded me of what matters: not perfection, but presence.

To **my mentors,** Those who challenged me, uplifted me, betrayed me, taught me, walked away, or walked beside me—thank you. Each of you shaped this story and the version of me I now share with pride. Every lesson, whether painful or profound, became a building block in this beautiful life I live and lead today.

To **my editor,** Carolyn—thank you for treating my story with tenderness and reverence. You challenged me to go deeper, pushed this book to be its best, and brought a level of heart and precision I'll always be grateful for. Your belief in this project—and in me—meant more than you know. I'm so lucky our paths crossed and even luckier to build beautiful things alongside you.

To **my designer,** January—your art gave this story a soul. Thank you for bringing such intuitive creativity, care, and intention to every detail. You didn't just make this book beautiful—you made it *feel* beautiful. I'm so grateful for your patience, your vision, and your spirit. I am truly humbled to consider you a soul sister!

And finally, **to you,** The reader who picked up this book and chose to walk this path with me—thank you. Thank you for your openness, your courage, and your willingness to show up—not just for this story, but for your own. My deepest hope is that something within these pages sparked something within you. May you remember that you were never broken. You were always becoming. And may your presence light the way for others, just as you've allowed mine to reach you.

From my heart to yours,
Michelle Marie King

About the Author

Michelle Marie King is a force of nature—Founder and CEO of Positive Presence Global, the largest life coaching company for teens and young adults, and a visionary leader reshaping the future of mental health, mentorship, and generational healing.

Since 2015, Michelle and her team have walked alongside thousands of young people and their families, serving as a lifeline through darkness, a mirror to their worth, and a catalyst for their transformation. Their work is not about fixing—it's about helping those who are ready, remember who they truly are.

But before she became a mentor to the masses, she had to become a lifeline to herself. A former international runway model and pageant queen, Michelle's early life was defined by performance, perfectionism, and the pursuit of external validation. It wasn't until the birth of her daughter, Savannah, in 2015, that everything shifted. What began as "model coaching" to teen girls evolved into a global mission to awaken worth in the hearts of the entire next generation.

Today, Michelle is a nationally acclaimed speaker, world-renowned social entrepreneur, and positivity activist who has raised millions for mental health and youth empowerment causes. Her voice—raw, radiant, and relentlessly real—has earned her a reputation as one of the most trusted and transformative mentors of our time.

Her debut memoir, Made of Magic, is more than a book. It's a movement. A powerful reflection on brokenness, resilience, and rising. A soul-stirring reminder that pain doesn't weaken us—it initiates us into our power. Michelle lives in Minnesota with her husband, Adam, and their daughter, Savannah. Her mission is unapologetically bold: to eradicate teen suicide globally by 2035—and to help every person she meets rise in their truth, their worth, and their light.

Michelle Marie King
Blue Talon Photography